Praise for
Code in Every Class

"Kevin and Ria's call to action—for teachers to integrate computer programming into their curriculum—is a challenge we can confidently take on with all of the resources shared in *Code in Every Class*. From rationales to resources to lesson plans, this book has all the support you need to inspire your students."

—Lisa Highfill, teacher, co-author
of *The HyperDoc Handbook*

"*Code in Every Class* is the perfect book for any teacher, administrator, or even parent hoping to bring coding into their students' lives. The pages are filled with compelling reasons to answer the 'why' and easy-to-implement lessons to answer the 'how'!"

—Jennie Magiera, educator and
author of *Courageous Edventures*

CODE
In Every
CLASS

How All Educators Can
Teach Programming

Kevin Brookhouser, M.Ed.
And
Ria Megnin

Code in Every Class

These books are available at special discounts when purchased in quantity for use as premiums, promotions, fundraising, and educational use. For inquiries and details, contact the publisher: edtechteam.com/press.

Published by EdTechTeam Press
Cover design by Genesis Kohler
Editing and Interior Design by My Writers' Connection

Paperback ISBN: 978-1-945167-21-8
eBook ISBN: 978-1-945167-22-5

Irvine, California

Join the conversation!

EdTechTeam Global Google + Community:
community.codeineveryclass.com

KevinBrookhouser.com

#codeineveryclass

Dedication

This book is dedicated to the students and teachers who are using technology to open the world for *all* people—no exceptions.

Contents

Foreword

Coding is instructing and problem-solving to make the technologies surrounding and connecting us do fun and important things—ultimately to transform how people live, play, and work.

—ANDREW STILLMAN

Initially, my writing an introduction for Kevin and Ria's book didn't make sense. After all, *Code in Every Class* encourages non-experts to shed their inhibitions and mental blocks, and adopt computer-programming learning standards into their teaching. Writing the foreword didn't make sense, because I'm considered by many to be an expert programmer. I'm a veteran science teacher and school administrator who coded a handful of scripts and add-ons for Google Apps. These time-saving teacher tools (Doctopus, Autocrat, Formmule, etc.) were adopted by tens of thousands of tech-forward educators in the early- to mid-2010s, and their unexpected success gave me small-time EdTech notoriety and, eventually, led to securing the position of Chief Product Officer at Amplified IT. Currently, I lead a team of software developers who create tools extending the Google Apps platform to reimagine how work is accomplished in schools.

As the rare teacher who mutated into a software developer, I understand how easily I could get cast into the caricature that the authors rightly argue is a key enemy of progress in computer science education: the socially-off-kilter math types who, unlike *normal* people, just "get" computer science. I understand the temptation of believing coding is an elite domain for the "geeks" because, from my vantage point, computer science always appears to come more naturally to *others* than it does to me.

But as I considered this further, I thought, *Who better to write a foreword for this book than someone who could be aptly described as one who simply has a talent for sustained mental effort and attention?* The authors compare this talent to Carol Dweck's concept of "grit." Trust me, there's no genius here. I was just a mid-career educator with middling intellectual talents, driven enough to invest thousands of hours into teaching myself to become a less and less mediocre software engineer—largely via books, the Internet, passion projects, and fighting back the demons of self-doubt. Likely, my stubbornness is the only remarkable thing about me. After reading and reflecting on *Code in Every Class*, I'm certain the habits of mind leading to my success with learning computer programming later in life were actually rooted in my primary and secondary education.

As a middle-class kid born in the late 1970s, I was privileged to have role models at school and in my personal life, particularly women, who were committed to computer science education. After working as an occupational therapist for more than a decade, my mother returned to school to earn a master's degree in computer science and launched a second career in IT project management at IBM. Largely because of her, I always had access to computers.

With the Cold War raging, NASA running at full bore, and the *A Nation at Risk* report beating the drums of educational urgency, all students at my well-funded public elementary school in the suburbs of New York City spent several hours a week on Commodore 64s in the computer lab. We learned Logo through self-paced coding activities, programming digital turtles to draw geometric figures and the maps of the countries of the world. My high school pre-calculus teacher, Mrs. Barbara Sarver, had been a computer programmer before becoming an educator and used programming to illustrate pre-calculus concepts. She also taught an elective BASIC and Pascal course I took, and when some of us wanted to take a second year of programming, the school arranged for us to take evening classes at Pace University. Coincidentally, our professor was my mother's favorite professor, Dr. Alan Stix, who had a special talent for making abstract ideas accessible to a diverse, multi-generational night school crowd.

Although the computational literacies and attitudes I gained in my primary and secondary years would eventually contribute to my love of computer science, they *did not* lead me to study computer science in college in the early 1990s. Perhaps because the Internet and mobile devices hadn't quite rocked the world yet, I found computer science to be uninspiring in its real-life applications, and other passions claimed my attention. I realize now that what I took for granted then would later provide the critical underpinnings and confidence to transition from a career in education to one in software development. I also understand now that these computational literacies have been a powerful medium for professional growth, self-expression, and joyful invention—akin to reading, writing, and arithmetic in shaping the opportunities and intellectual pleasures I have known thus far in life. *Code in Every Class* is fundamentally about creating these same opportunities and connections for all students.

Code in Every Class sagely warns against the "coding-genius" caricature and dispels any notion teachers might have about needing to spend thousands of hours developing deep expertise in computer science before teaching it. Kevin and Ria rightly point out that these needless hang-ups prevent many teachers from taking simple, highly achievable steps to introduce their students to the joys and power of coding.

Kevin and Ria—essentially both novices of computer science—carefully unpack some of the mental and historical baggage discouraging teachers from treating coding like another basic literacy. Additionally, they explore the social factors that have led (and continue to lead) to an astounding lack of gender, racial, and socioeconomic diversity in the technology professions. They believe educators, and society at large, have mythologized computer programming as elite, highly specialized knowledge, as opposed to a universally necessary fundamental. The authors sound the call for teachers to lead the way in introducing *all* students to coding with the same priority they would give reading, writing, and arithmetic. While teachers aren't expected to be masters of all literacies (*e.g.,* we don't expect primary school teachers to be expert mathematicians), Kevin and Ria argue teachers shouldn't fear learning computational thinking skills alongside their students. In fact, they champion this open stance toward lifelong learning to be an essential behavior for teachers to model for their students.

Given the fact that technology is radically changing our world, this is truly an exciting time for teaching young people to be comfortable with this new currency of economic and social power. Coding has become a wizardry for our times, offering up transformational spells—and economic security—to those willing to master its skills and mindset. The smallest breakthroughs can be extremely motivating, and once you get into the debugging mindset, you and your students will feel your grit growing by the minute.

If you follow Kevin and Ria's advice and open your learning stance to coding, I suspect you and your students will discover why I came to love programming so much I made it my second career. Coding is instructing and problem-solving to make the technologies surrounding and connecting us do fun and important things—ultimately to transform how people live, play, and work.

What could be more delightful?

Andrew Stillman
Chief Product Officer, Amplified IT

Authors' Note

Thanks for picking up (or downloading) a copy of *Code in Every Class*! We're glad to have you on board as we work with educators to change the world—one student at a time.

Kevin has two of the best jobs in the world: teaching high school students at the innovative York School in Monterey, California, and traveling the globe to lead sessions on technology in the classroom for EdTechTeam (*edtechteam.com*).

EdTechTeam is a Google for Education Professional Development Partner. Cutting-edge, world-changing ideas come alive at its workshops and conferences. One of those ideas began to emerge in 2014 when Kevin noticed two interesting trends with his new session *Build Your Own Android Apps* and *Learn to Code*: few people signed up, and those who did were absolutely wild about it.

Ria also has two of the best jobs in the world: writing about the people and places making a difference in education today and teaching creative writing and other skills to adults and high school students. She and Kevin met when she wrote several articles about York School for *The Salinas Californian* newspaper in 2005.

In 2014, we completed our first book collaboration, *The 20time Project: How Educators Can Launch Google's Formula for Future-Ready Students*, which shares Kevin's approach to project-based learning. After receiving great feedback for *20time*, we decided to dive into another book on today's education scene, this time about teaching technology. We dreamed up the concept for *Code in Every Class: Why All Students Need Computer Science and How All Teachers Can Provide It*. Our goal is to demystify the world of programming so teachers can help their students discover its wonders.

While working on *Code*, we've seen how important technology education can be. The schools, community centers, and even churches around us are adopting digital tools at an incredible rate. Just one example is Ria's adopted city of Dayton, Ohio, that has embraced a culture of tech innovation, welcoming techies of all ages and backgrounds to maker fairs, drone and robotics events, summer camps, and coding clubs—including a few that focused on helping minorities and women excel in this expanding field. Several area school districts have adopted 1:1 Chromebook programs. Dayton even has a tech-themed "maker" bar downtown where patrons can rent 3-D printers, soldering stations, and host geek game nights! Computer science is reinvigorating this Rust Belt community and others like it around the country. We're seeing the world evolve even as we write about it!

Aside from the fun and exploration it offers, technology opens doors of opportunity. Our core premise is that tech-empowered students will have far more well-paying career options available to them, regardless of geography. Those same students will bring the value of diverse voices and experience to the world because of technology.

An extraordinary team, including Holly Clark, Erin Casey, Andrew Stillman, and EdTechTeam, helped this book come together. Their guidance, expertise, and enthusiastic embrace of this project have made the book immeasurably better.

York alum and entrepreneur Dan Long provided invaluable background and insights from the world of tech and business.

Google Apps Certified Trainer and Google Certified Teacher John Sowash helped Ria understand the role and potential of technology in education today.

Kevin's wife, Beth, continues to prove her superhero status. When she is not saving two adorable boys from scratched knees with healing kisses, she's saving homeless animals at the SPCA for Monterey County.

Ria's husband, Adam Megnin, has been a keen supporter and sounding board, lending his technical expertise, curiosity, and encouragement throughout the work.

We must also offer a special thanks to Sam, Wally, Lilly, Johnny, Teddy, Ori, Nova, and Quinn—our very favorite young learners and proto-engineers.

We also have to give a nod to the technology used to create this book. During the two-year process of developing *Code in Every Class*, we met face-to-face only once. Otherwise, all of our work was conducted using Google Drive, FaceTime, Hangouts, and smartphones. We find it fitting that a book on technology and twenty-first century learning was created almost entirely through virtual collaboration.

Finally, a special thank you to all of the educators dedicated to creating the best possible learning environments for your twenty-first century learners. May this book help you put a dent in the universe.

Kevin Brookhouser and Ria Megnin

How to Read This Book

Every school has the "techie" teacher. You know, the one who's always talking about "Apple this" and "Google that" and always carrying around a new gadget. If you're *that* teacher, great! You'll get a lot out of this book. But if you're *not* that teacher—if computers and tech devices make you feel a little (or a lot) uncomfortable—you may get even more out of this book. We wrote it so you don't have to be uncomfortable any longer.

Code in Every Class is about keeping technology, and specifically code writing (aka programming), as simple as possible. We'll share the basics about what programming is, provide you with resources and links to excellent tech education tools and communities, and include lessons that you can scale up or down based on your comfort level and your students' expertise.

None of the tools and practices you'll learn about in this book will require the major commitment of time, energy, and practice becoming a coding expert takes. Good thing, too, since teachers don't have time for that; we're in the education business! So unless you're planning to switch fields and become a computer programmer, a few hours with this book should give you what you need to be an effective guide for young tech learners in your classroom.

With this in mind, here are a few suggestions for getting the most out of *Code in Every Class*:

Don't feel you have to read from cover to cover! Skip around. Flip through the chapters. Find something interesting and read more. Jump right to Chapter 9, *Lessons,* pick a lesson, and try it with your classroom. Or go straight to Chapter 7, *Build Your Expertise*, open your computer, and play!

Open up your computer and play! Diving in and exploring is the best way to learn about coding and technology.

Build your resources and connections. Because including information about all of the available educational technology tools and solutions in one book would be impossible, consider *Code in Every Class* a guide and launching point—not your final source on bringing coding into your students' lives. We've dropped links to dozens of online resources and communities into the book and compiled a Resources appendix at the back. Check these out and get connected with the world of EdTech learning, connection, and discovery.

Join the conversation. Get engaged on Twitter using the hashtag *#codeineveryclass* or join the EdTechTeam global community page on Google+. By tapping into these communities, you will get classroom-tested ideas and support from fellow educators, and you can share your own successes. We can't wait to see you online!

Introduction

Every student in the twenty-first century needs experience in coding—not just the kids who might be considered typical computer "nerds"—but *every* student! Coding is a fundamental skill to open the world in ways we are just beginning to imagine.

Code in Every Class is all about making universal lessons in coding happen.

Don't panic! Teaching coding doesn't mean you have to devote hundreds of hours to becoming a certified tech geek! Our goal is not to teach you or your students to become a programmer. Our goal is for every teacher to modify at least one lesson to include some aspect of computer programming. That's it!

One lesson might not seem like much, so why is it so important? We live in a world with an infrastructure founded on technology. We need students who know how tech works—which demands that we make sure they understand code and the computational thinking involved with it. If we don't prepare them, they're going to miss out on many of today's opportunities.

< Coding Terms > ───────────────

Coder, computer programmer, developer, computer scientist ...

All of these terms describe people who write instructions computers follow. "Coder" has emerged as the popular term for enthusiastic beginners, although traditionally it refers only to the assembly-line staff member who follows instructions to bring programmers' or developers' design vision to life.

In this book, we'll use the terms *coding* and *programming* interchangeably because we're promoting both beginner level computer language skills and the higher level computational thinking essential for the twenty-first century.

A World Built On Computing

Coding extends far beyond computers with keyboards and screens. Programming controls every vehicle, television, phone, airport terminal, baby monitor, furnace, traffic light, and checkout station. Coding coordinates the systems delivering electricity, shipping food and goods around the world, providing security, and helping perform surgeries.

Consider the career landscape. Modern agriculture relies more on machine programmers and computer-based administrators than on actual field labor—and this reliance will only increase. Well-paying manufacturing positions require expert knowledge of robotics and computer processing. To thrive, any small business owner must be able to use a smartphone, social media, and spreadsheets to engage with clients and deliver what they need. From music to art to film, the entertainment industry relies on programming and design. Corporate leaders must capitalize on tech-based communication, innovation, and potential, and grasp what's happening under the hood of technology in order to imagine what's needed and manage the people hired to make it happen.

Beyond the work world, understanding computer science is a fundamental part of democratic citizenship. To stay well-informed and connected, vet the onslaught of media, and make rational decisions, we need to understand the processes involved in issues and elections. This requires understanding the major roles played by technology in polling, voter database management, electronic voting systems, statistical analysis, and social media. And a solid grounding in logic-based thinking doesn't hurt either!

Computer technology impacts every aspect of society. In fact, most people keep at least one tech device on them at all times. But for some unfathomable reason, basic computer science has not yet risen to the same level as the other essential subjects in education. When it comes to tech—one of the most important elements of modern life—we still don't require students to know anything about how it works!

Granted, this oversight doesn't happen out of malice. No one's sitting in an ivory tower saying, "Children must be kept ignorant of technology engineering." For the most part, educators simply don't believe they have the knowledge or qualifications to teach it. Or we think tech education doesn't belong in the classroom alongside traditional subjects.

It's time to change the way we think!

Computer Labs Are Not Enough

A few lucky students *are* exposed to computer science and programming in the classroom as, across the United States and around the world, educational teams are transforming curricula to include more computer programming classes. And change is happening fast! In 2013, only twelve states counted computer science toward high school graduation math or science requirements. Today, that number is up to thirty states, plus Washington, D.C.[1] Still, only one in four American schools offers a computer science class.

Even if every kindergarten through twelfth-grade student took a formal course in computer programming, it would not be enough to truly empower them. Computer classes are taught in separate computer labs—an archaic approach when technology can be used to enhance so many classroom and daily life activities. Imagine letting students learn to write only in a high school elective writing course—and not allowing them to bring a notebook or pen to their other classes. This is essentially what today's technology education method does.

The good news is many schools are getting on board with basic computer literacy and the incorporation of technology into the curriculum as the presence of Chromebooks, iPads, smartboards, and other classroom tech tools grows. The era of the computer as separate from education is over. Computers are being integrated into every class—history, math, English, art, biology, physics—as they should be. Students are constantly using computers to access information, create projects, collaborate, solve problems, etc. They're practicing skills upon which the "real world" relies.

We believe educators have a responsibility to go a step further and help students truly understand the potential of these tools.

- How do iPads actually work?
- What is a database, and what rules govern it?
- What are computer languages, and what difference does it make to use SQL or FORTRAN?

These questions don't belong in an obscure techie class. These questions are applicable to the careers our students will pursue and the daily tasks they will perform. Our job is to bring technology out of the lab and incorporate computer literacy into our regular subject lessons in relevant and meaningful ways.

---

1   "Promote Computer Science," CODE, *code.org/promote*

The Revolutionary Classroom

Becoming as revolutionary in the approach to technology education as teachers are in teaching core subjects will help bridge the gap. Rather than letting politicians and curriculum bureaucrats hold the technology education movement to a slow trickle, the world needs teachers to lead the charge. Our desire is for *all* teachers in *all* classes to teach some of their content using computer science techniques. The biggest hurdle, of course, is that most teachers *don't know how*. Very few school staff, faculty, or administrators have a computer programming background—even the *techies*! Even fewer are trained to share their coding knowledge with kindergarten through twelfth-grade students.

Fortunately, we've discovered that the most effective learning happens when we flip the traditional educational model, which required teachers to be the experts, and instead allow students to explore, research, discover, test, and create their own solutions. Today we know students learn better when they are challenged by real-world problems—including ones that haven't been solved yet. In this new model, teachers aren't standing at the front of rows of desks dispensing answers. Instead, we serve our learners as guides, helping them find the information, resources, and support they need to achieve their goals. We are there to point students in the right direction, help keep them on track, and encourage them along the way. Meanwhile, we are learning right alongside them.

In other words: Our students take the lead, and we discover the answers together.

And *that* is how we can all start to teach tech.

< Shared Learning >

Technology is the perfect subject for exploring the collaborative learning model. The entire tech world is built on this approach. Even rock-star computer program developers rely heavily on Internet forums, articles, videos, and blogs to research solutions. Developers are constantly seeking, sharing, and collaborating in niche communities.

This open-source, idea-sharing engagement helped create modern technology and continues to foster tech innovations today.

Kevin's Classroom

Kevin here. Many of you probably support the idea of teaching technology without having to be credentialed experts but are wondering if it can actually work.

Absolutely, it can work—I have firsthand experience to prove it! I am definitely *not* a computer programmer. In fact, my teaching career began in history and English, and even though I have always used technology as part of my lessons, I didn't always challenge students to explore those tools more deeply. According to the traditional approach to education, technology wasn't something to teach in English!

But in the summer of 2010, I attended the Google for Education Certified Innovator program. After setting foot on Google's mind-blowing campus, I realized the world had utterly transformed and computer science was driving the changes. I wanted my students to be prepared for their future, but even more, I wanted them to help *create* their future. And to create, they had to know not only how to use computers, but how to make them work.

When I returned to school, I didn't ask permission to change the curriculum, and I didn't create a huge shift in my classroom. I simply changed one of my creative writing lessons during the year to involve playing with some computer logic. I got a few raised eyebrows from students expecting a more traditional English project, but I figured there was no reason my students had to learn Shakespeare the way I did twenty years ago. Just as the outside world has changed dramatically since the 1980s, so should the classroom experience transform.

And the project worked—my students got fired up about technology *and* Hamlet! I started incorporating computer science opportunities into more of my lessons, learning and experimenting right along with my classes, and watching their interest surge.

Pretty soon my colleagues at York School in Monterey, California, got excited about the approach and began adopting it. Today, York offers cross-curricular projects where students—from subjects ranging from art to Spanish to code and design—collaborate on meaningful work, such as an interactive project exploring the experience of Central American immigrants making the journey north to America.

Granted, none of us are experts, but there's no question all of our students are now getting very strong art, language, and tech skills.

A Guide for Today's Classrooms

Code in Every Class is a book for educators—by educators. We'll go in depth about the importance of sharing coding experiences with all K–12 students—why it's so valuable for their careers, their citizenship, and our global and local communities. We'll also consider the impact teaching computer science to students—who might otherwise be stuck in cycles of intergenerational poverty—has on social justice.

Along the way, we'll address some of the most common concerns raised about universal coding education, including concerns of educators who may have little to no personal experience with coding and computer science. Believe me: Whether you're a teacher, administrator, or parent, you *do* have the skills and tools required to teach coding technology—even if all you have is chalk on a playground.

Finally, we'll share simple and enjoyable ways to explore coding at every age and skill level. We'll walk through the process of launching a coding program and preparing lesson plans appropriate for each grade level. You'll find dozens of resources to draw from and share with your students and colleagues, including online programs, good old-fashioned printed books, and supportive communities of fellow educators.

We're so excited to share the value of coding and tech exploration for all students because we see the immediate and long-term impact. Schools that have embraced this philosophy are building communities of enthusiastic learners who produce life-changing projects for themselves and their neighborhoods. They're graduating lifelong learners who build meaningful, productive experiences at colleges and in their careers.

We're confident you'll come away from *Code in Every Class* enjoying a transformative relationship with technology. So let's dive in!

<1>

THE CASE FOR CODING

A Chance to Shine

During my students' (and my) first endeavor with coding we used Code.org as our basis, beginning with the various modules in Code Studio. My students quickly understood the basis of programming and how the blocks made the figures on screen perform certain tasks.

One student in particular (let's call him Mike) stood out. Mike was a student with severe learning disabilities, and school had been very challenging to him. However, something about coding clicked with him—he was the first student to complete the first three levels in the program. Suddenly, others were flocking to him for support! The look in his eyes spoke volumes. Here was a student who usually had to ask others for help, and he was the one helping them.

To me, this is one of the greatest benefits of coding—it can level the playing field for all students and give each a moment to shine, all while teaching valuable skills.

—*Justin Birckbichler, EdTechTeam community*

Everyone knows coding is a valuable skill for *some* people. We've all seen the stories about young computer programmers—Bill Gates, Steve Jobs, Mark Zuckerberg, and Elon Musk—growing up to run the world. But we believe coding is a valuable skill for *all* students—not just the "computer geeks." Justin's story above is one of our favorites, in part because we know so many kids like Mike who fall in love with coding and may grow up to be full-time computer programmers. But this isn't the main reason we celebrate their success.

We celebrate because coding prepares kids for a wide range of careers—not just jobs in computer science! Whether they dive into hardcore, back-end computer programming or apply their knowledge of code and technology to creating music, art, and community projects, young adults comfortable with computer tools and the possibilities offered by computational thinking have a tremendous advantage in their chosen fields. On a global level, the big problems we face—climate change, economic inequality, global terrorism, health care—will have to be solved, at least in part, by computer programmers and data crunchers!

The Great Leveler

We believe in exposing all students to coding because it gives them so much more than simple computer skills. Students are thrilled to realize the devices they use each day have a design and instructions they can control—and they are empowered. They start to play around, tweaking and creating to fit their own needs. Instead of being passive consumers, students begin using technology to connect with their communities and help others. These experiences then make them highly desirable in a job market where comfort with technology and innovation gives people better opportunities to earn a good living for themselves and their families. For this reason alone, teaching coding can be the single greatest leveler of the education playing field.

> ## CODING PREPARES KIDS FOR A WIDE RANGE OF CAREERS—NOT JUST JOBS IN COMPUTER SCIENCE!

We'll dive into this idea more deeply in the next chapter, where we'll talk about the demand for coders and other computer science positions and the importance of preparing our future workforce for them. For now, let's look at why—since coding experience is so valuable—only one in four U.S. schools teach programming to their students.[1] We've found six major misconceptions keeping coding out of the classroom today:

1. Only programmers can teach coding.
2. Students already have too much screen time.
3. Only future programmers benefit from code in school.
4. Coding doesn't fit the curriculum or testing regimen.
5. Technology changes too fast to teach.
6. Teaching computer science is too expensive.

Misconception #1:
Only Programmers Can Teach Coding

The major roadblock to teaching coding is very few of today's educators grew up learning what makes calculators, electronics, and other devices tick. But here's the thing: Coding is simply *the process of creating logical instructions.* All we have to do is define a problem and break the solution down into logical, step-by-step instructions a machine can perform.

---

1 *code.org/promote*

For instance, you can't simply tell a robot: "Go to the cafeteria." Coders must use literal, logical, step-by-step instructions to translate the mission of going to the cafeteria into a process the robot can successfully follow:

- Move forward five tiles.
- Open classroom door.
- Move forward two tiles.
- Turn ninety degrees to the right.
- Move forward fifty tiles.
- Turn ninety degrees to the right.
- Open door to cafeteria.
- Move forward two tiles.

Unfortunately, knowing the logic behind programming doesn't alleviate the underlying fears so many educators have about teaching it. First, there's the fear of breaking the traditional educational culture. We remember the schools we grew up in and naturally tend to recreate the same model for our students. So it's a big leap for most of us to start teaching technology which simply wasn't part of the K–12 curriculum we experienced. But if we want our young graduates to have a successful career and life, we've got to expand beyond traditional basics to reflect the world these kids will live and work in.

An even bigger fear is losing our sense of authority. We are comfortable being the experts at the front of the class, standing above our captive audiences and bestowing upon them the accumulated knowledge of our years. (Our students are comfortable with this, too, and may not be thrilled about a change!) To turn this model upside down and introduce a topic we know almost nothing about is legitimately scary—especially since we're guaranteed to have students who know more about technology than we do.

But if we are going to prepare students for their futures, we need to wholeheartedly embrace this new dynamic because it's the only way for education to continually progress in our constantly, rapidly transforming world. Learning is now a perpetual and collaborative practice, where everyone is required to continually take on new skills. Today, teaching is centered around creating lifelong learners with well-developed skills in research, practice, and communication.

We teach our students to write, even though few of us are published authors. We teach mathematics, even though we're rarely mathematicians, accountants, or physicists. We teach the basics of science, social studies, and history without being full-time professionals in those fields. Similarly, our new role is to share what expert knowledge we do have and model curiosity about what we don't know. Ask questions we don't know the answers to. Collaborate with our kids. "Hey, here's a problem I don't know how to solve. Let's work together to find a solution." Abandon the lonely post at the front of the room! Exploring new ideas and technologies alongside our students teaches them critical twenty-first century skills.

Coding is an excellent place to start this shift because it's simple enough that anyone with a little bit of basic math and an open mind can do it. Showing students the relevance of what they're learning is also easy: Everywhere they look, something is being driven by code. Coding gives them a sense of potential control over the devices dominating their world. Also, plenty of resources make basic-level computer programming both easy to learn and incredibly fun. Dozens of websites offer interactive learning games for new coders of all ages, capitalizing on the growing awareness in education that play is a powerfully motivating learning tool. Computer coding, after all, is just playing with logic! And we educators can draw on thousands of local and global clubs, camps, and community programs to get expert-level support on any topic. These resources are growing in response to our tremendous need for more computer training.

So when the fear about tackling coding in your classroom rears up, take a deep breath and do it anyway. The next generation needs you.

< What Is Computer Programming? >

What is computer programming? It's simply problem-solving!

Step 1: Identify and explore a problem.

Step 2: Create a sequence of operations (algorithms) to address the problem.

Step 3: Test the algorithms for accuracy and performance.

Step 4: Turn them into source code using a programming language.

Step 5: Test, debug, maintain, and improve the code. (This is also known as software development.) For instance, a teacher wants to spend less time grading. She decides the biggest time sink for her is calculating overall grades, and the best way to decrease the time involved is by using a formula in a spreadsheet to automatically weigh and calculate each grade. She sets up a series of spreadsheet formula operations to fetch the grade data for each student and assignment, multiply each data point by its assigned weight percentage, calculate the totals, and automatically generate each student's final grade with every newly entered data point. After testing to make sure the formula works accurately, she uses it for each class's spreadsheet, checking every few weeks to make sure it's still working properly.

That's coding!

Misconception #2: Students Already Have Too Much Screen Time

We know how frustrating and heartbreaking it can be to see kids zoned out on a violent video game or distracted by apps on their phones. When we walk into a crowded space where it seems like everyone's looking down at a screen and waiting for a notification, it appears dystopian.

Because today's devices are designed to stay on constantly and continually deliver content, they're absolutely more addictive, more distracting, and more likely to harm our relationships with others than other forms of media delivery. No one wants an entire generation lost in uncontrolled, self-absorbed, meaningless activities.

But none of this means we should ban screens during class time. Would we ban textbooks because kids read comic books? Just because they both use paper and ink doesn't mean they offer the same experience.

If computers in the classroom are causing students to be constantly distracted, it's not a technology problem; it's a management problem. We've seen classes with zero technology and zero engagement because students pass notes, read under their desks, or just stare out the window daydreaming. We've also seen classrooms where every student has a device, and every student is totally engaged. Technology is neither the barrier nor the catalyst for student growth. Their growth depends entirely on how we use technology.

> TECHNOLOGY IS NEITHER THE BARRIER NOR THE CATALYST FOR STUDENT GROWTH.

< *How To De-distractify*
Your Classroom >

1. Have dedicated screen-down time.
2. Issue harder challenges.
3. Ensure what you want students to learn is relevant to their lives. (Hint: Good rap music composition requires an understanding of metrical verse, coding loops, and social context.)
4. Give students the opportunity to be creative while working.
5. Pay attention to the distractions of choice and why they're so popular. Leverage them for learning! Maybe you need a class Instagram account.

The way to develop thoughtful, healthy, compassionate citizens is not to ban new technologies from the classroom, but to give students the power to use them *well*—including knowing how and when to turn them off. Teaching students the mystery behind these seemingly magical devices helps transform them from handheld dictators into creative tools. In fact, one of our biggest responsibilities as technology educators is to show our students how to use tech to build better relationships and give value to our world. Well-designed technology can support mental health, life skills, emotional well-being, and community building. Instead of surrendering to the waves of technology and drifting along with whatever they're given, students who understand the basics of programming can become wizards who do good!

Here's where coding comes in. It gives our students a totally different way of engaging with technology. While users flit into and out of apps, games, and online conversations, programmers must dedicate their attention to long bouts of code crafting, multi-level problem-solving, extensive research into online articles and forums, and deep collaboration—an intensely creative process almost completely opposite the surface-level, mindless consumption we discourage.

For instance, I (Kevin) lead a class at York School where students build Android apps using MIT's Android App Inventor. One of my students developed a first aid app users can launch when they witness a victim of a medical emergency. The app asks the user a series of questions and directs them to call 911 and provide treatment. Another student built an app to help people identify and eliminate invasive plants. I make sure I have both those apps with me when I hit our local trails.

My students are thrilled to upload the software they've built and watch their devices follow their commands! This incredibly empowering experience can and does lead to systems able to solve the world's most wicked problems.

So don't hesitate to incorporate computers into some of your lessons. However, it's a good idea to discuss healthy device usage. Share tips and tools to help make your tech experiences positive. Though students may spend most of their free time on smartphones or tablets or game consoles, they rarely know how to use them to create instead of consume. They need help to safely and respectfully engage with social media, search for online information, and tweak their devices and apps to boost productivity and health. Our tech-saturated kids need our guidance to learn boundaries and healthy engagement with the devices filling their lives.

< Check Assumptions >

It is important to remember that many of our students are *not* oversaturated by technology. Many families can't afford smartphones, tablets, computers, or Internet access in their homes. Judicious access to devices in class and after school can help level the playing field and ensure that all students can compete when it comes to the technology their future employers will expect them to understand and use.

Misconception #3: Only Future Programmers Benefit from Code in School

Imagine teaching addition only to the handful of high school *math nerds* who take it as an elective, and then being surprised by a shortage of accountants. The accounting world isn't the only thing affected if students aren't exposed to basic math. Likewise, more than computer programming jobs are at stake when students aren't exposed to coding.

The skills involved in basic coding and tech literacy carry over into every job and every task of daily life. They help people make informed, logical decisions, especially regarding areas heavily influenced by technology: the economy, medicine, the environment, education, politics, international relations, etc. Additionally, students exposed to coding have the ability to use technology to promote civic engagement and advocate for those without a voice.

Teaching coding is really about teaching *thinking*. Students who code understand complex problems are rooted in much smaller issues, which they can tackle with creative problem-solving and computational thinking. Exposure to computer programming teaches students the correlation between what they put *into* something and what they

> TEACHING CODING IS REALLY
> ABOUT TEACHING THINKING.

get *out* of it. They learn that every outcome can be traced back to some earlier input. This grounding in logic helps fight the allure of pseudo-science, the false messages of marketing campaigns, and the temptation to believe something just because it is exciting and popular. In addition to logic, students learn other thinking skills such as creative problem-solving. Coding also teaches students how to:

- Recognize patterns
- Derive meaning from abstract symbols
- Develop logical strategies for tackling challenges
- Build and test algorithms
- Practice troubleshooting
- Follow complicated steps to a conclusion

By giving students the tools to gather information and organize it in meaningful ways, computer science empowers them to tackle the problems of the world. Whether they're building a simple budget-tracking spreadsheet for a class field trip, developing a nature website for the neighborhood, or creating a mobile app to help local residents find their pets, coding helps our kids translate their ideas into reality—one line of logic at a time.

> ### < Major Aspects of Computer Science >
>
> **Logic** is formal, structured thinking about problems. Examples include abstraction, Boolean logic, number theory, and set theory.
>
> **Algorithms** are general strategies toward solving problems. They include methods such as divide and conquer, recursion, heuristics, greedy search, and randomized algorithms.
>
> **Information theory** is the exploration of what information (or data) is, how to represent it, and how to use it to model the real world.
>
> **Systems theory** allows us to create complex systems to address a problem's requirements and constraints.
>
> **Artificial intelligence** is any exploration of replicating human thinking. (Scientists are currently focused on machine learning, computer vision, and natural language processing.)

Misconception #4:
Coding Doesn't Fit the Curriculum or Testing Regimen

The need to meet state and federal curriculum standards while pushing our students to pass standardized tests is one of the worst pressures on educators today. Understandably, teachers are much more reluctant to introduce new content when they barely have time to teach what's already mandated. However, you might want to take a second look at introducing coding as a way to meet those mandates.

The Common Core State Standards Initiative doesn't specify a curriculum. It simply requires that public school students across the United States learn the knowledge and skills they'll need to succeed. And since it does not attempt to define lesson plans or instructional methods, teachers have an awesome opportunity to incorporate coding into their classes. In fact, many of my public school colleagues have concluded that giving students the autonomy to pursue ambitious, independent projects incorporating coding might be the best way to meet the priorities of the Common Core. Other Common Core standards that coding can help achieve are the following:

Mathematics
 Geometry
 Measurement and Data
 Statistics and Probability
 Operations and Algebraic Thinking

English Language Arts / Literacy
 Key Ideas and Details
 Integration of Knowledge and Ideas

Incorporating coding is as simple as choosing any project from our regular curriculum and adding a computer programming component. For example:

- To practice **geometry**, elementary students could program a sprite (a digital character moveable on a screen) to draw different polygons.
- To identify **key ideas and details**, elementary students could program a robot to navigate an obstacle course depicting a story's main events.
- To demonstrate **measurement and data**, middle school students could collect temperature recordings from different continents throughout the year and use spreadsheet formulas to analyze the information.
- To explore **probability**, middle school students could design Android apps to roll digital dice.
- To integrate **knowledge and ideas**, high school students could build a website taking visitors on a virtual field trip to all the locations of Shakespeare's plays, complete with video clips of the class performing its favorite scenes.
- To exhibit **algebraic thinking**, high school students could develop branching-logic apps to help customers at the local animal shelter choose a new pet.

Use the curriculum guidelines for your classroom outcomes as a framework to inspire student innovation—rather than as a straitjacket keeping them from meaningful engagement with their world.

< The Benefits of K—12 Experience with Coding >

Learning to code instills in students the core twenty-first century skills our education system currently lacks and desperately needs: creative problem-solving, persistence, collaboration, and critical thinking. Coding develops a strong foundation of logical reasoning and, even better, lets students learn these skills in an environment modeling empowerment, delight through play, and entrepreneurialism. Coding also offers significant tangible results:

- Students achieve autonomy with technology.
- The playing field is leveled for students from even the most disadvantaged backgrounds.
- Students receive access to some of the most high-demand, high-benefit twenty-first century careers.

Misconception #5:
Technology Changes Too Fast to Teach

Technology changes fast.

Personal computers and smartphones evolve massively every couple of years. Health tech is exploding with new tools for genetic analysis, high-resolution real-time brain scans, and 3-D printed organs. Energy tech is creating new fuel cells, bioelectric sources, and sustainable energy models every month. Transportation technology is turning the dreams of self-driving cars, Hyperloop trains, and viable missions to Mars into reality. Faced with this rapid rate of change, it is natural for teachers to feel that preparing students for the future is nearly impossible when we can barely imagine where technology might take us in the next two or three decades.

The good news is—the *what* actually isn't important. Sure, Google Drive, iTunes, and Facebook play huge roles in our daily lives today. But will they in ten years? Our own teachers didn't require us to draft blog posts before personal web pages existed, learn Boolean logic for future Google searches, or write music for the age of auto-tune. They simply gave us the basics and encouraged us to adapt to and solve problems along the way.

Our students will adapt, too, using the computer science principles we teach them to engage with emerging technologies. So teach your kids how to learn new things. Equipped with a growth mindset, they can evolve right along with twenty-first century computer science.

Misconception #6: Teaching Computer Science Is Too Expensive

Thirty years ago, technology was expensive. When we were kids, an Apple IIe with 64 KB of memory was a massively powerful dream machine costing several thousand dollars. Today, kids can learn coding on a 512,000 KB Raspberry Pi Zero, a credit-card-sized computer which processes information one thousand times faster than the Apple IIe. And the Zero sells for—wait for it—only five dollars! In fact, used laptops with all the peripherals can be found for as little as one hundred dollars. For a little more than two hundred dollars, schools and families can purchase a fully functional Chromebook running Google's lightweight, yet powerful, Chrome Operating System. Even the tiniest school districts are getting help from big donors to ensure their students don't miss out on the tech revolution. Organizations from Washington, D.C. to the Silicon Valley to local chambers of commerce are willing to chip in.

And software? Google's suite of products—Docs, Sheets, Slides, Drawing, Forms, Earth, Maps, Gmail, etc.—are available at no cost. Most coding platforms and tutorials are free, and many other programs have low-cost workarounds. As long as you have some way to access the Internet, you and your students can get what you need to deliver strong computer science content without spending a dime.

The cost of maintaining a school's tech fleet is also becoming easier and more affordable. Laptops are sturdier; upgrades are less disruptive. An entire fleet of Chromebooks can be set up for one-click security and online update management, with support and educational resources from Google Apps for Education to make it easy for newbies to keep their classroom tech on target. In short, don't let concerns about cost hold your school or classroom back. Technology investments present a very low-entry barrier.

But what if your school doesn't have devices or Internet access? You can *still* teach computer science because the principles of coding and digital literacy can be taught in many forms! Check out some tech-free lessons in Chapter 9 or find a library and visit *code.org/curriculum/ unplugged* to view a host of non-electronic learning adventures.

Teach Entrepreneurialism with Coding

Having responded to the most common misconceptions of bringing code into your classroom, we'll close this "case for coding" by exploring one more core twenty-first century skill: entrepreneurialism. An

> CODING IS AN IDEAL TOOL FOR TEACHING KIDS THE THREE CORE ELEMENTS OF ENTREPRENEURIALISM: DELIGHT, EMPOWERMENT, AND INNOVATION.

entrepreneur takes the initiative to create effective solutions to real-world problems. All of our students need this skill.

Our education system, developed in the nineteenth and twentieth centuries to prepare a workforce for manufacturing and office pools, is not designed to teach entrepreneurial thinking. But as demand grows for creative engineers, innovative marketers, visionary leaders, and even service-industry workers who stand out from the crowd, the tide of education is turning. More schools are integrating future-ready learning practices into their curriculum. Politicians are working with educators to change the counterproductive focus on test scores in education. Colleges are accepting holistic portfolios as admission criteria instead of college entrance exam scores alone.[2]

Teaching coding is one of the easiest ways we educators can contribute to this shift. In fact, coding is an ideal tool for teaching kids the three core elements of entrepreneurialism: delight, empowerment, and innovation.

Delight

While we have so many reasons to bring computer programming into every classroom, the number one reason is joy. Computer programming can be an incredibly joyful creative adventure, and we want all teachers and students to experience the joy of watching a program they created come to life.

We're also discovering that the delight of play is crucial to learning.[3] Computer coding is essentially *playing* with logic. As we'll see in later chapters, we don't teach coding with boring tech manuals anymore! We have hundreds of ways to make it incredibly fun.

2   Scott Jaschik, "Admissions Revolution," Inside Higher Ed, September 29, 2015. Retrieved from *Insidehighered.com/news/2015/09/29/80-colleges-and-universities-announce-plan-new-application-and-new-approach*

3   Rachel E. White, "The Power of Play: A Research Summary on Play and Learning," Minnesota Children's Museum Smart Play, September 2015. Retrieved from *mcm.org/wp/wp-content/uploads/2015/09/MCMResearchSummary1.pdf*

Empowerment

Forcing students to regurgitate memorized content for machine-based tests does *not* empower them. This outdated approach to education no longer serves our workforce, and it has never served the world when it comes to solving serious problems.

Entrepreneurialism requires a completely different approach—an approach that combines creative, collaborative, project-based learning while integrating multiple subjects as students seek meaningful solutions to real-world problems. Instead of learning information for the sake of memorization and repetition, students will learn to seek out information and resources needed to solve challenges. What they will discover along the way will have context and purpose, giving their brains a deeper, longer-lasting understanding.

Coding encompasses this creative, collaborative, project-based problem-solving. Imagine asking students to design and program a robot to clean up the stream behind their school. Or develop a spreadsheet to track fundraising and budgeting for the year-end field trip. Or build a website documenting local bicycle accident reports, community interviews, and videos in order to convince community leaders to install bike lanes in the neighborhood. All these can be done through coding. Now that's empowerment!

Innovation

Our society operates on the myth that adults know everything that matters. We perpetuate this myth by testing students to make sure they learn what adults know. The truth is, the world is changing much too fast for anyone to be a know-it-all expert about anything. If we insist on having to know everything, we leave no room for developing or discovering new approaches to unexpected challenges.

So be vulnerable. When you share basic skills, allow kids to test potential new applications so they're not just rehashing already-solved problems. When you teach about the latest developments in technology or in your field, show them innovative approaches are both fun and crucial.

Coding can be our greatest tool for innovation. As with any other creative tool, students first need to learn to use existing programming languages and structures. Once they get the hang of it, though, their potential is unlimited. Some may go on to invent drones to measure carbon dioxide levels at high altitudes, or satellites to track endangered species, or rockets to redirect dangerous asteroids. By encouraging students to break old patterns and find innovative ways to do what's always been done, coding gives them the power to change the world.

‹2›

THE DEMAND FOR CODING

Want to help your students get a great job?

Businesses from your local coffee shop to tech giants are hungry for workers with strong computer science skills. In June 2016, The Conference Board research group reported more than half a million American job openings in the "computers and math" industry.[1] These jobs appear in every industry and every state, and they pay much better than average. According to the U.S. Bureau of Labor, a high school graduate working as a computer support specialist earns, on average, $51,470 a year[2]—about $15,000 more than the median income for *all* Americans, regardless of education.

But it gets better. With a bachelor's degree, an entry-level network and computer system administrator averages $73,000 a year. Earnings only go up from there for full computer programmers, database administrators, information security analysts, computer network architects, and software developers who can earn well over six figures!

---

1   "The Conference Board Help Wanted Online," The Conference Board, June 2016. Retrieved from *conference-board.org/data/helpwantedonline.cfm*

2   "Occupational Outlook Handbook: Computer and Information Technology Occupations," Bureau of Labor Statistics, December 17, 2015. Retrieved from *bls.gov/ooh/computer-and-information-technology/home.htm*

Of *Glassdoor.com*'s list of the top twenty-five highest-paying job categories, ten are in computers and information science.[3]

In addition to salaries, benefit packages are equally strong. A sizable portion of technology positions falls under the government's umbrella, offering some of the best benefits and worker protections available today. Private sector businesses also offer generous incentives to attract quality workers.

But the tech industry is still headed for trouble. All the high pay and benefits in the world can't attract a nonexistent skilled workforce. And it's not likely to exist for some time. We're not training nearly enough students to compete for these high-wage, high-benefit jobs. More than three out of every four of these jobs require at least a bachelor's degree in computer science or information technology, says Maggie Johnson, Google's director of education and university relations. Yet the United States only produces 16,000 computer science undergraduates each year.[4] As a result, young graduates with experience in computer science are almost guaranteed jobs with salaries high enough to pay off their student loans within a few years.

> OF GLASSDOOR.COM'S LIST OF THE TOP TWENTY-FIVE HIGHEST-PAYING JOB CATEGORIES, TEN ARE IN COMPUTERS AND INFORMATION SCIENCE.

---

3   "25 Highest Paying Jobs In Demand," Glassdoor, February 17, 2015. Retrieved from *glassdoor.com/blog/highest-paying-jobs-demand*

4   Maggie Johnson, "The Computer Science Pipeline and Diversity: Part 1—How did we get here?" Google Research Blog, July 8, 2015. Retrieved from *googleresearch.blogspot.com/2015/07/the-computer-science-pipeline-and.html*

< *Jobs, Jobs...Everywhere Jobs* >

The U.S. Bureau of Labor is quite optimistic about careers in the computers and information science field.[5] According to a Bureau report from December 2015, computer and information technology jobs will likely grow twelve percent over the coming decade, from about 3.9 to 4.4 million jobs. The Bureau says this is due "to a greater emphasis on cloud computing, the collection and storage of big data, more everyday items becoming connected to the Internet in what is commonly referred to as the 'Internet of things,' and the continued demand for mobile computing."

Accompanying the Bureau's report, this chart describes major job categories in the computers and information science field, along with basic descriptions, general educational requirements for the positions, and the median pay for U.S. workers in these positions in 2015.

OCCUPATION: Computer Support Specialists	
JOB SUMMARY: Computer support specialists provide help and advice to people and organizations using computer software or equipment. Some, called computer network support specialists, support information technology (IT) employees within their organization. Others, called computer user support specialists, assist non-IT users who are having computer problems.	**ENTRY-LEVEL EDUCATION:** High School Diploma/GED
	2015 MEDIAN PAY: $51,470

---

5 "Occupational Outlook Handbook: Computer and Information Technology Occupations," Bureau of Labor Statistics, December 17, 2015. Retrieved from *bls.gov/ooh/computer-and-information-technology/home.htm*

OCCUPATION: Web Developers	
JOB SUMMARY: Web developers design and create a website and are responsible for the look of the site. They are also responsible for the site's technical aspects, such as its performance and capacity, which are measures of a website's speed and how much traffic the site can handle. In addition, web developers may create content for the site.	**ENTRY-LEVEL EDUCATION:** Associate's Degree
	2015 MEDIAN PAY: $64,970

OCCUPATION: Network and Computer Systems Administrators	
JOB SUMMARY: Computer networks are critical parts of almost every organization. Network and computer systems administrators are responsible for the day-to-day operation of these networks.	**ENTRY-LEVEL EDUCATION:** Bachelor's Degree
	2015 MEDIAN PAY: $77,810

OCCUPATION: Computer Programmers	
JOB SUMMARY: Computer programmers write and test code that allows computer applications and software programs to function properly. They turn the program designs created by software developers and engineers into instructions a computer can follow.	**ENTRY-LEVEL EDUCATION:** Bachelor's Degree
	2015 MEDIAN PAY: $79,530

OCCUPATION: Database Administrators	
JOB SUMMARY: Database administrators (DBAs) use specialized software to store and organize data, such as financial information and customer shipping records. They make sure data is available to users and are secure from unauthorized access.	**ENTRY-LEVEL EDUCATION:** Bachelor's Degree
	2015 MEDIAN PAY: $81,710

OCCUPATION: Computer Systems Analysts

JOB SUMMARY:
Computer systems analysts study an organization's current computer systems and procedures and design information systems solutions to help the organization operate more efficiently and effectively. They bring business and information technology (IT) together by understanding the needs and limitations of both.

ENTRY-LEVEL EDUCATION:
Bachelor's Degree

2015 MEDIAN PAY:
$85,800

OCCUPATION: Information Security Analysts

JOB SUMMARY:
Information security analysts plan and carry out security measures to protect an organization's computer networks and systems. Their responsibilities are continually expanding as the number of cyber-attacks increases.

ENTRY-LEVEL EDUCATION:
Bachelor's Degree

2015 MEDIAN PAY:
$77,810

OCCUPATION: Software Developers

JOB SUMMARY:
Software developers are the creative minds behind computer programs. Some develop the applications allowing people to do specific tasks on a computer or another device. Others develop the underlying systems running the devices or controlling networks.

ENTRY-LEVEL EDUCATION:
Bachelor's Degree

2015 MEDIAN PAY:
$100,690

OCCUPATION: Computer Network Architects

JOB SUMMARY:
Computer network architects design and build data communication networks, including local area networks (LANs), wide area networks (WANs), and intranets. These networks range from small connections between two offices to next-generation networking capabilities, such as a cloud infrastructure serving multiple customers.

ENTRY-LEVEL EDUCATION:
Bachelor's Degree

2015 MEDIAN PAY:
$100,240

OCCUPATION: Computer and Information Research Scientists	
JOB SUMMARY: Computer and information research scientists invent and design new approaches to computing technology and find innovative uses for existing technology. They study and solve complex problems in computing for business, medicine, science, and other fields.	ENTRY-LEVEL EDUCATION: Doctoral or Professional Degree
	2015 MEDIAN PAY: $110,620

So where are all these jobs? You might be surprised to discover the Silicon Valley is *not* the busiest geek space these days. Instead the largest groups of techies can be found in government and business hubs around the world, from Washington, D.C. to New York City, Seattle, Chicago, Atlanta, London, Seoul, Johannesburg, Rio, and anywhere else a group of corporate headquarters can be found. Small cities and towns have plenty of tech opportunities as well, especially if they're home to a college or university. They also tend to have less competition and a lower cost of living. Of course, the tech industry can also be perfect for people who enjoy telecommuting. Imagine earning San Francisco salaries while paying only Midwest rent!

For an example of what a young software engineer might find when seeking a job, review this LinkedIn listing[6] for a mid-sized company in the D.C. region in July 2016:

Job Description

Position is responsible for performing requirements analysis, design, coding, testing, verification and validation, and maintenance of enterprise custom desktop and web-based solutions for editing and reporting on geospatial databases with links to legacy systems. Responsible for

---

6   linked.codeineveryclass.com

developing software code to standards, meeting require-ments on schedule and with minimal defects, while also assisting in test development. This role involves work-ing within a software support team in a collaborative environment.

Qualifications
- Minimum of three years related experience or a B.S. in Computer Science or Engineering
- C#/C++ (C++ may be school only, or a strong willing-ness to learn)
- Web Technologies (CSS, HTML, JS, jQuery)

Did you notice a bachelor's degree is optional as long as the appli-cant has three years of related experience? They're even willing for the candidate to learn C++ on the job.

This company offered an extensive list of benefits, including health insurance, vacation, and a 401K. Salary wasn't mentioned, but *glass-door.com* reported the national average for software engineers in July 2016 was $95,195.[7]

Our students will benefit from learning technology regardless of what type of career they pursue. A solid understanding of how data is organized can mean the difference between working in door-to-door sales and being hired as a marketing analyst. Restaurant managers who use apps and social media campaigns to attract customers have more job security than those who rely on traditional advertising. Even if they never touch a device on the job, people trained in computational thinking are better equipped to help their companies with inventory, online security, automation, systems design, and data management. For twenty-first century careers, knowing tech pays off.

---

7   *glassdoor.com/Salaries/software-engineer-salary-SRCH_KO0,17.htm*

> # FOR TWENTY-FIRST CENTURY CAREERS, KNOWING TECH PAYS OFF.

The Dark Side of Coding

Good pay and benefits aren't the only reasons people are attracted to computer and information science industries. Besides spending less time and money on formal education, computer programmers also tend to enjoy other enviable benefits:

- flexible hours and location
- playful work environments that encourage creativity and innovation
- solid opportunities for professional growth
- a sense of autonomy
- the intangible reward of working on projects to make the world better

But there's a dark side to programming as well. The hours may be flexible, but they're often long and irregular. Intense deadlines are common. Programmers are much more likely to serve as temporary contractors than union-protected employees. Not only could their job disappear after a few months, their entire company might burst onto the scene and vanish before the health benefits kick in. However, the demand for programmers gives good performers strong leverage at the negotiating table and rebound potential after a layoff.

Another challenge is the most hardcore computer scientists must deal with the frustration of months of mind-numbing, repetitive, line-by-line coding and troubleshooting. In fact, this is one of the prime arguments against universal coding in the classroom. Critics point out that successful developers need to be unusually persistent and detail-oriented people who love researching and problem-solving.

Don't be discouraged! First, these aren't necessarily inherent traits; they're skills to be strengthened. But they won't be if students aren't exposed early. Second, teaching coding to all students is not about turning them into programmers. It's about turning them into people comfortable with making technology work for them.

Where Are All the Coders?

The lack of highly qualified programmers is a major factor slowing down technology development across industries.[8] The shortage is driven by lack of exposure and early support in the tech talent development funnel. With few opportunities for learning, playing, and engaging with role models in the field (ideally, role models who look like them), most young people of the past few generations simply haven't realized a computer technology career might be for them.

As a result, we have a critical shortage of skilled computer scientists and a field overwhelmingly dominated by "nerds"—the stereotypical socially inept white or Asian male genius who toils obsessively at mind-numbing tasks in back rooms. This stereotype makes programming careers seem both unattainable and undesirable. While it is true that computer programming requires some qualities commonly viewed as *nerdy*—hyperfocus, attention to detail, and a seeming obsession with learning all things technological—many of these valuable qualities can be learned without being taken to extremes.

---

8   John Dodge, "The war for tech talent escalates," *The Boston Globe*, February 19, 2016. Retrieved from *bostonglobe.com/business/2016/02/19/the-war-for-tech-talent-escalates/ejUSbuPCjPLCMRYIRZIKoJ/story.html*

> ## < What Does It Take to Be a Programmer? >
>
> A good computer programmer needs the following skills:
>
> - extraordinary attention to detail
> - the ability to focus on and prioritize multiple tasks under intense deadline pressure
> - the creativity and persistence to see a complicated project through many months of development and troubleshooting
> - strong math and problem-solving skills
> - excellent memory for data
> - the ability to organize and manage projects
> - strong program design and data structure skills
> - familiarity with common algorithms and code libraries
> - the ability to assess and integrate a project's elements, including hardware, interface, programming, databases, etc.
> - awareness of the constantly evolving field of computer science

We must change the story around programming if we want more students to succeed. The jobs are available—our job is to prepare the workforce. As we teach coding in our classrooms, we're preparing our students. What a wonderful way to grow our tech workforce to meet the world's needs!

<3>

CODING AS SOCIAL JUSTICE

From Silicon Valley to London, Tel Aviv to Hong Kong, tech jobs are dominated by white and Asian men. In the United States, this group comprises 84 percent of science and engineering professionals—including computer scientists.[1] Most experts agree that the lack of gender and ethnic diversity is due to two main factors:

- systemic problems in the educational pipeline, and
- patterns of hiring and promotion bias in the industry.

Jane Margolis explains in her book *Unlocking the Clubhouse: Women in Computing*, that white and Asian boys of upper-middle class backgrounds share specific tech advantages:[2]

- They are most likely to be exposed to computers at an early age.
- They often have family and community members working in computer technology.

---

1   "Women, Minorities, and Persons with Disabilities in Science and Engineering: 2013." (2013) National Center for Science and Engineering Statistics Directorate for Social, Behavioral and Economic Sciences, National Science Foundation. Retrieved from *nsf.gov/statistics/wmpd/2013/pdf/nsf13304_digest.pdf*

2   Margolis, Jane and Fisher, Allan. *Unlocking the Clubhouse: Women in Computing*. MIT Press, Cambridge, Mass., 2001.

- They see media portrayals of people like themselves in the tech field.
- They are most likely to be seen by educators as potential computer scientists.

This combination of exposure and bias effectively turns girls, children of color, and children from lower-class backgrounds away from the tech field. That's roughly 70 percent of America's school-age population!

Certainly, this is a serious situation with serious consequences. We know computing and data industry jobs offer better pay and benefits than most career fields, especially for the level of education required. We also know demand is strong and rising. Focusing only on white and Asian boys not only blocks a huge number of people from finding successful employment, it prevents our tech industry from growing to meet the needs of customers and the world.

Fortunately, the patterns are starting to shift. High-profile tech firms recognize they have a diversity problem, and they're making efforts to attract, hire, and promote a much more diverse workforce. Addressing the diversity problem is not just good policy, it's excellent for tech companies' bottom lines. Bringing in different life perspectives helps them better understand their customers, provide tools and services to meet their real-life needs, and bring in more business.

Looking at how the tech industry reached this point can give us a better sense of how to move forward.

The Boys' Club of Computer Geekdom

You might be surprised to learn that in the early decades of computing, women made up the vast majority of computer programmers. They worked as hands-on coders, performing the complex yet repetitive tasks of designing and delivering instructions for the new machines to process. Despite the advanced mathematical skills involved, most of the tasks were considered clerical, assigned to low-wage "women's work." Men were assigned the "real" work of building the machines, from designing the circuits to constructing the equipment. As computers became more effective and widespread, computer experts in the 1960s and 1970s developed a "distinctively masculine identity," computing history researcher Nathan Ensmenger argues, "in which individual artistic genius, personal eccentricity, anti-authoritarian behavior, and a characteristic 'dislike of activities involving human interaction' were mobilized as sources of personal and professional authority."[3]

The new culture had a profound effect on women's participation. Girls growing up in the 1970s received a clear message: computers are for geeky boys.[4] Advertising and media coverage of the tech industry began to focus on boys and men, and Steve Jobs and Bill Gates became the skinny white male superheroes of computing.

This pattern fed on itself. Most computer learning systems and video games were designed and marketed to appeal to boys and meet the needs of a male-dominated geek culture. Fewer girls were attracted to the tech world. Those who did faced a *boys' club* mentality. Colleges and businesses played out the cultural bias, failing to recognize the talents of coders who didn't fit the geek-boy model.

These messages matter. Girls Who Code reports that 74 percent of middle-school girls express interest in STEM fields; however, a few years later, only 17 percent of AP Computer Science test takers are high school girls. When these high school girls select college majors, only 0.3 percent choose computer science. Yet researchers have found gender differences in technology disappear when girls and boys are given

3   Nathan Ensmenger, "Beards, Sandals, and Other Signs of Rugged Individualism: Masculine Culture within the Computing Professions," *The University of Chicago Journals*, Osiris 2015 30:1, 38-65.

4   Laura Sydell, "The Forgotten Female Programmers Who Created Modern Tech," *All Things Considered Morning Edition*, National Public Radio (NPR), October 6, 2014.

the same opportunities to practice and learn. For instance, in 2007, a team of researchers from the University of Toronto discovered playing an action video game for ten hours virtually eliminated the gap in spatial attention and mental rotation ability between men and women.[5]

Even so, there *are* real differences in how boys and girls approach technology. A two-year research project published in 2000 by the American Association of University Women found "girls approach the computer as a 'tool,' useful primarily for what it can do; boys more often view the computer as a 'toy' and/or an extension of the self. For boys, the computer is inherently interesting. Girls are interested in its instrumental possibilities, which may include its use as an artistic medium." [6]

> # RESEARCHERS HAVE FOUND GENDER DIFFERENCES IN TECHNOLOGY DISAPPEAR WHEN GIRLS AND BOYS ARE GIVEN THE SAME OPPORTUNITIES TO PRACTICE AND LEARN.

---

5   Jing Feng, Ian Spence, and Jay Pratt, "Playing an Action Video Game Reduces Gender Differences in Spatial Cognition," Psychological Science, Vol. 18, No. 10. (2007): 850–855.

6   American Association of University Women. "Tech Savvy: Educating Girls in the New Computer Age." AAUW Educational Foundation Commission on Technology, Gender, and Teacher Education. (2000) Retrieved from *history.aauw.org/files/2013/01/TechSavvy.pdf*

< *Damaging Stereotypes* >

As Janet Shibley Hyde and Marcia C. Linn found in their 2009 meta-analysis of gender in mathematics and science education, differences in the way boys and girls approach—and are approached with—technology can lead to girls being shut out of tech education and careers.

In general, most young boys build and explore; play with blocks, trains, etc.; and engage in activity and movement. For a typical boy, a computer can be the ultimate toy that allows him to pursue his interests, and this can develop into an intense passion early on. Many girls like to build, play with blocks, etc. too. For the most part, however, girls tend to prefer social interaction. Most girls develop an interest in computing later through social media and YouTube, girl-focused games, or through math, science, and computing courses. They typically do not develop the intense interest in computing at an early age like some boys do—they may never experience that level of interest.

Thus, some boys come into computing knowing more than girls because they have been doing it longer. This can cause many girls to lose confidence and drive during adolescence with the perception that technology is a man's world. Both girls and boys perceive computing to be a largely masculine field (Mercier 2006).[7] Furthermore, there are few role models at home, school, or in the media changing the perception that computing is just not for girls.

---

7   E. M. Mercier, B. Barron, and K. M. O'Connor, "Images of self and others as computer users: the role of gender and experience," *Journal of Computer Assisted Learning*, Stanford University, 22: 2006, 335–348. *life-slc.org/docs/ Mercier_etal-Imagesofself.pdf*

> *This overall lack of support and encouragement keeps many girls from considering computing as a career.[8]*
>
> *In addition, many teachers are oblivious to or support the gender stereotypes by assigning problems and projects that are oriented more toward boys, or are not of interest to girls. This lack of relevant curriculum is important. Many women who have pursued technology as a career cite relevant courses as critical to their decision.[9, 10]*

8   "Women Who Choose Computer Science—What Really Matters," Google, May 26, 2014. Retrieved from *docs.google.com/file/d/0B-E2rcvhnlQ_a1Q4VUxWQ2dtTHM/edit*

9   Carrie Liston, Karen Peterson, Vicky Ragan, "Evaluating Promising Practices in Informal Information Technology (IT) Education for Girls: Phase III: Women in IT—Survey Results," National Center for Women and Information Technology / Girl Scouts of the USA, 2008. Retrieved from *ncwit.org/sites/default/files/legacy/pdf/NCWIT-GSUSAPhaseIIIReport_FINAL.pdf*

10 Johnson, M. "The Computer Science Pipeline and Diversity: Part 1 - How did we get here?" Google For Education Blog, July 8, 2015. Retrieved from *googleforeducation.blogspot.com/2015/07/the-computer-science-pipeline-and.html*

The problems continue in college where role models, mentors, and classmates tend to be overwhelmingly male. Research by the American Association of University Women[11] shows undergraduate women studying computing face the following obstacles:

- undergraduate classroom teaching in which the "weed-out" practices and policies that favor competition over cooperation tend to advantage men
- laboratory climates in which women are seen as foreign and not belonging at best, and in which they experience blatant hostility and sexism at worst
- well-meaning people who unwittingly create stereotypes by reminding students that "women can do computing as well as men"
- strong resistance to changing the system in which these and other subtle practices are continuously reproduced

Where extracurricular support exists, women and minority students often turn it down because they fear being seen as someone who needs "extra help." This keeps them from building peer networks other students take for granted. It is not surprising, then, that in the first decade of the 2000s, the percentage of computer science bachelor's degrees awarded to U.S. women dropped from 27.6 percent to just 17.7 percent.

Beyond the Ivory Tower

The challenges for women in tech continue beyond the world of education. A 2015 *Forbes* piece cites a report by Kieran Snyder, a former senior leader at Microsoft and Amazon, who interviewed 716 women who held tech positions at 654 companies in 43 states. On

---

11 American Association of University Women. "Tech Savvy: Educating Girls in the New Computer Age." AAUW Educational Foundation Commission on Technology, Gender, and Teacher Education. (2000) Retrieved from *history.aauw.org/files/2013/01/TechSavvy.pdf*

average these women worked in tech for seven years and then left. Kieran asked these women specifically why they opted out.

> Some 192 women (27 percent) cited discomfort working in these companies. The overt or implicit discrimination was a primary factor in their decision to leave tech. That's just over a quarter of the women surveyed. Several of them mentioned discrimination related to their age, race, or sexuality in addition to gender and motherhood. They also stated that lack of flexible work arrangements, the unsupportive work environment, or a salary that was inadequate to pay for childcare all contributed to their decision to leave.[12]

Still, women are making progress in the computer and information processing industry. In its November 2015 issue, *WIRED Magazine* reported that women comprise 24 percent of tech employees in Silicon Valley today. Former Hewlett-Packard CEO Carly Fiorina, Meg Whitman (Fiorina's successor), Facebook COO Sheryl Sandberg, and Yahoo! CEO Marissa Ann Mayer have all become household names in recent years. Recognition of female pioneers of early technology—from Ada Lovelace to Admiral Grace Hopper—is also growing. And while most television shows and movies continue to show girl geeks as awkward anomalies or, worse, love interests for the real techies, at least they're being shown.

Diversifying the Tech World

As hard as it is for girls to see themselves belonging to tech culture, it can be almost impossible for people who aren't of white or Asian background. As with women, the lack of role models has an early and damaging effect on young people of color. Additionally, a 2015 study by *WIRED Magazine* showed while 9 percent of the computing degrees

---

12 "Bonnie Marcus, "The Lack of Diversity in Tech Is a Cultural Issue," Forbes.com, August 12, 2015. Retrieved from *forbes.com/sites/bonniemarcus/2015/08/12/the-lack-of-diversity-in-tech-is-a-cultural-issue/#445b1ddb3577*

in 2012 went to black and Hispanic graduates, only 2 percent of Silicon Valley's techs are black and 3 percent are Hispanic. In other words, the tech workforce fails to reflect the diversity of the applicants coming out of our schools.

Janice Cuny, who directs the Computer Education program at the National Science Foundation, told *USA Today* that black and Hispanic candidates too often go completely unnoticed by tech companies. "There are these subtle biases that make you think that some person is not what you're looking for, even when they are."[13]

Race and gender aren't the only diversity challenges facing the computer industry. As Jane Margolis describes in her book *Unlocking the Clubhouse: Women in Computing*, white and Asian boys of upper-middle-class backgrounds have been the children most likely to

- be exposed to computers at an early age,
- have family and community members working in computer technology,
- see media portrayals of people like themselves in the tech field, and
- be seen by educators as potential computer scientists.

Socioeconomic factors have an even bigger impact than race or gender on young people's interest in pursuing STEM education and careers. While girls and people of color rarely see themselves represented in technology fields, children growing up in poverty rarely even see personal computers in their homes. Those who do have regular access to a computer—often through schools or libraries—face an even greater challenge. Studies exploring how people from wealthy and impoverished backgrounds use technology show a disturbing trend. When granted access to computers, children from poor neighborhoods tend to use them without adult guidance. They tend to jump

---

13 Elizabeth Weise and Jessica Guynn, "Tech jobs: Minorities have degrees but don't get hired," USA Today, October 13, 2014. Retrieved from *usatoday.com/ story/tech/2014/10/12/silicon-valley-diversity-tech-hiring-computer-science-graduates-african-american-hispanic/14684211*

from program to program, giving up when frustrated or confused. Those who persist tend to play non-educational games, watch videos, or listen to music, encountering significantly fewer words on the screen than their wealthier peers. Finally, disadvantaged kids tend to engage in more drill and practice than creative or innovative activities when using tech tools for academics.[14]

Beyond providing simple access, it's critical for schools to offer young people guidance on how to engage with technology, which is why incorporating code instruction in every class, for every subject and age group, is so important. After all, if only wealthy white and Asian boys are exposed to technology and protected from bias in the field, then more than two-thirds of America's school-age population is being steered away from the tech field! And this number increases when children with physical, emotional, and learning disabilities are counted—many of whom could greatly benefit from exposure to technology career opportunities.

The Benefits of Creating Change

What a loss when kids don't believe tech is for them! But the fact is, students who don't get technology developmental opportunities aren't likely to pursue degrees in those fields. And unfortunately, this is just the beginning of tech diversity issues.

When tech jobs go disproportionately to middle-class white and Asian men, less diversity goes into how technology is designed and the problems technology can address. Women and men tend to have very different approaches to working through problems. The same is true for people raised in different cultures—or whose life experiences and learning perspectives aren't part of the traditional mainstream,

---

14 Annie Murphy Paul, "Educational Technology Isn't Leveling the Playing Field," Slate, June 25, 2014, Retrieved from *slate.com/articles/technology/future_tense/2014/06/neuman_celano_library_study_educational_technology_worsens_achievement_gaps.html*

upper-middle-class America that most techies come from. The new perspectives shared by diverse staff help companies identify the unique needs and resources of non-mainstream customers, which can open connections with new markets: women, people of color, people with disabilities, people with alternative learning styles, and other cultural, religious, and socioeconomic groups. A 2015 study by McKinsey & Company revealed that businesses with more women leaders earned more than their competition 15 percent of the time. Those with more diversity in race and ethnicity were 35 percent more likely to earn more than the national median.

Additionally, there's the social injustice impact. Tech-hiring patterns have consistently kept women and people of color out of the high-paying, in-demand jobs of the technology sector, making it harder for yet another generation of disadvantaged people to break out of poverty. Technology firms and IT departments are some of the best places to access steady work, a living wage income, and reliable health, family, and retirement benefits—all before earning any higher degrees. These elements are crucial for young women and people of color who are trying to break a cycle of family poverty. Getting nontraditional students excited about computer science—and welcoming them when they pursue it at school and in the workplace—opens up opportunities for further education, personal growth, and income.

How We Can Create Change

Fortunately, the tech sector is starting to embrace the challenge to change! Starting in 2014, tech giants including Google, Apple, Microsoft, Amazon, Intel, Facebook, and Twitter began releasing diversity reports, sharing the percentages of women and people of color who work in leadership or technology positions. These numbers helped launch a very public discussion of big tech's diversity problem. Leaders began speaking at press events and business symposiums about the need to recruit more women and people from a variety of cultural and socio-economic backgrounds. Conferences on minorities in tech sprang up throughout the region, and women's networks in the field surged.

Even better, businesses began addressing the benefits packages, company policies, and tech cultures focused on the needs of young, mainstream men. Human resources departments started to address cultural biases in hiring and promotions, providing better family leave and scheduling support, and addressing the "all-night work party" atmosphere that tends to shut out women, older workers, and other groups.

Still, the tech giants knew even the biggest changes at their companies would have only a small impact on the industry's demographics. The real work needed to happen much sooner. To cast a wide net as early as possible, companies began funding clubs, camps, afterschool programs, and nonprofits to perform educational outreach for girls and economically disadvantaged children. They also helped launch and promote Hour of Code, a global movement by Computer Science Education Week and *Code.org*, to share fun one-hour introductions to computer science and computer programming with millions of students worldwide. (Learn more and connect with some of the many organizations providing resources for girls, minorities, and other young coders by checking out our Resources guide at the end of the book!)

> ## BRINGING CODING TO ALL CLASSROOMS GIVES GIRLS, MINORITIES, UNDERPRIVILEGED STUDENTS, AND NONTRADITIONAL LEARNERS CRUCIAL EXPOSURE TO TECHNOLOGY.

This brings us to the classroom and several ideas we educators can use to help increase diversity in the tech world:

- Offer coding opportunities in every class, for all ages and subjects, to expose students to the possibilities of computing regardless of their background.
- Take a professional development workshop with *Code.org*. Every training includes a session on recognizing cultural biases and engaging less-represented groups in technology experiences.
- Recruit coders—older students, computer science majors at nearby colleges and universities, staff from local software firms or IT departments, and people in your social media and business networks—to visit your classes. Be intentional about inviting tech professionals who are women or people of color.
- Host an after-school event series welcoming families to come learn about tech from their children.
- Remember that some of the students who will benefit most from learning technology may have the least amount of access. Work with local and national sponsors to help grow your classroom resources, such as broadband Internet, access to software and online programs, and 1:1 devices students can bring home. Advocate for library and community center technology offerings.
- For any underrepresented students—girls, children of color, students with disabilities, etc.—help address any self-doubt by building opportunities for practice and service. Providing connections with local and international role models who reflect students' backgrounds can transform their lives.

Bringing coding to all classrooms gives girls, minorities, underprivileged students, and nontraditional learners crucial exposure to technology. Down the road, this early exposure can lead to far more of these underrepresented groups diving into high-paying, intrinsically rewarding technology career fields in computing and data management. Not only will these initiatives benefit your students, they will make a big difference for your school and for the local and global communities.

<4>

ALL EDUCATORS CAN TEACH CODING

F ear is the main barrier keeping our students out of the tech fields. But not their fear—*our* fear. Consider Kevin's story below.

Kevin's Classroom

When I started teaching technology to my English students, my biggest hurdle wasn't content—it was anxiety. During my very first lesson, I asked students to create a story in the style of a Choose Your Own Adventure™ book, posting each branch of the story as a series of web pages. For instance, if a reader clicked the option to send the main character into a cave instead of continuing through the woods, the next web page would show the character going inside the cave and discovering a treasure chest. The user would then get to choose between options of opening the chest or going further into the cave. And so on.

I knew just enough about coding to know this would be a great way to teach branching logic. But things got scary when some of my students asked to explore probabilities. They wanted to create some chance that when readers clicked to go into the cave, the character didn't find treasure, he found an angry bear. I had no idea know how to do that! I froze for about five seconds—then said, "Great idea. Go for it! But you're not going to find the answers with me. You're going to have to do some research to find them."

I felt super-weird having my students work on something I couldn't do myself. But they figured out how to make it work. (To this day, I'm not really sure how.) And boy, were they proud!

Occasionally, though, things don't turn out so well. Sometimes students get utterly stuck, and I can't help because I don't know enough about coding yet. In those cases, I work with my students to reassess their goals and find a different way to move forward on their project. While students may be disappointed, it's a chance for them to practice finishing a product rather than pushing for perfection. These times provide proof that students are working on projects and pushing just beyond their current limits—meaning they're growing!

The same thing happens when we risk teaching coding even though we're not coders. We push beyond our own limits—and we grow too.

The Scariest Lesson Is the First

So you're committed to teaching some tech even though you're not an expert. On the first day of school, your students will walk in, most of them not knowing how to code. Naturally, you may feel a little intimidated. How can you possibly bring these digital natives to the point where they feel actual control over their devices?

This is a good time to remind yourself that most kids don't know the alphabet or their numbers when they start school. Imagining them writing their own stories or managing family budgets is hard when they can't spell or add yet. So you start with the basics and you make it fun.

You can use the same approach with teaching coding to students: Do your best to make the topic enjoyable and safe to learn, and explore it together. Show them the exciting ways they'll be able to use what they're learning, both today and in the future.

> # DO YOUR BEST TO MAKE THE TOPIC ENJOYABLE AND SAFE TO LEARN, AND EXPLORE IT TOGETHER.

Initially, learning to code involves building fun projects and games within existing apps. Later your students will be able to create their own apps and games, build spreadsheets, program their own functions, and use their skills to work at amazing global businesses to help change the world. You can learn these skills right along with them, making great discoveries together along the way. When you are willing to learn technology alongside your students, you offer them three huge benefits:

- A model of curiosity, lifelong learning, and exploring together—showing them not knowing it all is okay. This can add tremendous energy to a lesson!
- Vulnerability to open up real relationships with kids.
- Student empowerment and practice with leadership, seeing problems as opportunities and creating solutions on their own. They're becoming critical thinkers and computer wizards at the same time.

Plus—it's fun!

We must abandon the notion we need to be the sole experts on what we teach, handing down knowledge to students like omnipotent gods. We already know, when it comes to technology, kids are always going to understand it better than we do. They are true digital natives—belonging to a world where technology dominates the culture—many of them steeped in devices and Internet access since birth. Instead of fighting the loss of authority, choose to embrace the opportunity to serve as a companion and guide, help kids imagine what's possible, and figure out the skills to make the possible happen.

How to Teach Coding When You Don't Know a Bit from a Byte

As we discussed in Chapter 1, most educators don't know how to code. Naturally, the idea of standing in front of a classroom of students and teaching programming feels terrifying, if not impossible—similar to teaching a foreign language we don't know. But this doesn't mean computer science is beyond the realm of our mortal K–12 educator understanding.

< The Myth of Programming >

From the 1970s through the late 1990s, only a small percentage of children had regular access to personal computers. Of this group, only a few were interested in studying the manuals to explore how and why computers worked. By the time these lucky kids—who must have preferred electronics to other activities—reached high school or college, where they had access to formal computer classes, they already understood a vast amount of technology. True beginners who joined these classes were at a huge disadvantage.

Computer programming was quickly seen as the realm of geeks with an inborn talent far beyond most people's reach—not to mention trouble making friends. The truth is, these coders simply had spent more time exploring technology and less time practicing social skills. Thus the myth of computer programming as an impossibly hard skill known only to uber-geeks was born.

The unfortunate consequence of this myth is the field became top-heavy with this group of people who had early access and encouragement to learn computers. The culture of education around computing reflected this, creating a steep learning curve and unwelcoming environment for anyone who didn't have similar experience or fit the "mold."

Today the experts-only, born-a-geek culture is under attack. Far more kids grow up with opportunities to play with technology. In fact, thanks to efforts like the Hour of Code movement (*hourofcode.com*), computer programming is one of the hottest areas in educational games. Thousands of fun, welcoming tools, classes, clubs, and online resources allow people to dive easily into coding, spawning a crop of kids who are eager to enter the computing world.

Teaching coding doesn't have to involve an actual computer. In fact, even if you have computers in your classroom, an important first step is to teach some coding without using them. As with teaching anything new, using familiar context and delivering it in a safe, no-fail, even playful way helps students learn. Plus it creates buy-in for students and confidence for you. This is also important because, while computers are very good at executing logic-based commands, the real work of solving a problem is done by the coders—a very human task. Coding without a screen establishes in our brains *we* are the creators.

Here's our favorite tech-free starter lesson: The Playground Coder. Your students will get to perform a series of basic commands—literally!

The Playground Coder

1. Grab some sidewalk chalk and have your students draw a 20x20 square grid on the pavement.

2. Students take turns being the "coder" and the "robot." The coder's job is to issue commands (forward, left, etc.). The robot follows the commands exactly. For example, if the coder says "forward seven," the robot moves forward exactly seven spaces.

3. Create tasks and challenge students to develop "programs" to complete it. For instance, tell students to draw a complete square. Their program would be: "Chalk down. Forward seven. Turn right 90 degrees. Repeat three times. Chalk up." Other task ideas are navigate a maze, write their names on the ground, and play tic-tac-toe. Find ways to relate these tasks to your curriculum.

4. Gamify things!

    a. See who can follow the most instructions in a row before forgetting a step.

    b. Who can use the fewest instructions to accomplish a task?

    c. Who can generate the most designs in a given time?

    d. Who can perform a program the fastest without mistakes?

    e. Play some music and program the "robots" to dance.

5. Take photos or video and celebrate what the class accomplished!

This exercise works for students in all grade levels. Even high school seniors enjoy getting outside and testing the limits of real-world programming and design.

And don't worry if instructions aren't followed exactly. Some of the best moments occur when things go wrong. For example, the programmer issues a command but forgets to add a number. The robot won't move—or might keep walking in the same direction right off the grid! Or there's a command to start hopping on one foot, but the robot kid is supposed to have her chalk down at the same time. It's *Simon Says* meets tech school! These instances create a great opportunity to teach kids glitches are a constant part of coding, and checking code and debugging can be fun. (Try handing out toy "bugs" when mistakes are made!)

The Playground Coder easily converts to classroom exercises such as the following:

1. Have students follow a "program" to write letters on paper, draw characters from history in crayon, or build a map.
2. Arrange desks to look like circuit boards, then use toy cars as electrical impulses and cardboard "switches" as logic gates.
3. Prepare no-bake cookies using a recipe as a program.

The goal is for students to better understand computational thinking. These basic coding exercises enable them to start breaking actions down into their smallest parts, and organizing using both logic and creativity—all without a single computer device.

Coding Instruction Made Easy

In the past few years, educational technology has simply exploded. Countless easy, fun, attractive programs are now available to teach beginners the basics of coding. The Hour of Code movement, for instance, has taught computer programming to more than one hundred million students worldwide. Its learning games feature familiar characters and worlds such as Star Wars, Disney films, and Minecraft, as well as video tutorials with celebrities and tech leaders, including women and people of color. And the field of fun coding sites for kids is growing every day!

This means teachers don't have to come up with their own coding lessons from scratch. We've included some great places to start in the Resources section at the end of the book.

But don't teach coding alone. Plug into the educational technology community. Reach out to potential community mentors, including recent graduates. Invite programmers and tech groups in your region to visit your classroom. Ask for help setting up an after-school club or a class project. You never know how those partnerships will grow!

One last note about adding coding in your classroom: You are going to look like a rock star. People will think you've unlocked one of the great mysteries of the universe! Use your experiences to bolster your résumé. Share what you know. Help spread the benefits of technology and computer science instruction to more classrooms and more school districts.

And remember that teaching our kids to code is not about teaching them to be computer programmers. It's about giving them the skills to change the world.

> TEACHING OUR KIDS TO CODE IS NOT ABOUT TEACHING THEM TO BE COMPUTER PROGRAMMERS. IT'S ABOUT GIVING THEM THE SKILLS TO CHANGE THE WORLD.

<5>
SPARKING STUDENT INTEREST

Kevin's Classroom

My students were trying to build a clock powered by a Raspberry Pi, but something wasn't working. I could see they were getting frustrated with their code, so I decided to video their process. They were struggling and struggling. Finally, they figured out what was wrong with the code, fixed it, and ran the program again. Success! See their joy here: codeineveryclass.com/pivid.

While it was thrilling to capture on video, their breakthrough experience is not a rare thing. Every single day that my students work through a computer programming task, they experience *eureka* moments and get frustrated, excited, thrilled, and delighted all at the same time.

The reality of coding is that my students sometimes get stuck. Every kid gets stuck, regardless of technical skill level. At some point, all students will need one-on-one technical or emotional attention and support. So I prepare my kids for this eventuality. I tell them, "You're going to go through really frustrating feelings. Don't personalize it. Those are feelings; they're not you. They're an inevitable part of the creative process, signaling that you're growing."

Naturally, they don't understand—yet. Later, when the frustration hits and they threaten to give up on their project altogether, I remind them: "As Seth Godin says, 'When you feel like you're stupid, that's when you're learning.'" And then they really get it. They latch onto the permission to struggle and reframe the tough times as motivation to persist. If they keep pushing but still can't succeed, we revisit their goals and find a creative way to rethink how they can be achieved.

Dealing with Fear

Whether they are total code beginners or amateur hackers, all students feel some performance anxiety. The sense of intimidation can be paralyzing, especially for middle school and high school kids. They fear looking foolish while learning—not being able to "get it" as fast or as well as the rest of the class. Or they fear doing so well that they're considered teacher's pets. Their fears surface in many ways—from subtle resistance to active self-sabotage to open battle with the teacher.

Our tests-focused education culture doesn't help this. Kids find out early which subjects they're "good at" and "bad at" when it comes to test time. This can kill their spirit of curiosity, exploration, and risk-taking—so much for creativity or learning new skills. When there's no room for failure, there's no room for growth.

Learning to code can both trigger fear and dispel it. Addressing potential fears directly gives students the tools they need to fight through their inner saboteur. Help your students understand that everyone is afraid of failure but that failures are *how* we learn, especially in coding.

The "Bad at Math" Myth

"I'm bad at math." This heartbreaking yet common sentiment is a direct consequence of our test-driven, performance-focused educational system. This same system has saturated our culture with messages like *math is hard* and *only nerds*—usually boys with glasses and lousy haircuts—*have great numbers skills*. These messages are lies and absolutely must be refuted. Math skills are fundamental for life:

- Students need financial literacy to understand which loans and investments are good deals.
- They need to understand statistics to make good decisions for their communities and share collective resources.
- Solid math skills let them make well-informed business recommendations. Confidence in those skills helps them to speak up when it matters.

Stress to your students the whole "bad at math" myth is patently untrue. Research conclusively shows math performance is determined by attitude. The truth is if people are willing to invest the time to learn and practice, they can master the math they need to thrive in this world.[1]

Many students avoid math like the plague, complaining it's boring or useless. Too often, they're right about it being boring! The traditional way of teaching math is to assign repetitive problems with no relevant context. Very often, the goal is simply to teach kids what's going to be on the test. Some of those skills may be revisited to solve a higher-level problem, but most are forgotten once the test is over. This assembly-line model of learning has led to generations of people wondering why we even bother to teach algebra or geometry, let alone calculus. How many times have you heard people say, "I haven't used that stuff since high school"?

---

1 Miles Kimball, Noah Smith, "The Myth of 'I'm Bad at Math,'" The Atlantic, October 28, 2013. Retrieved from *theatlantic.com/education/archive/2013/10/the-myth-of-im-bad-at-math/280914*

People don't learn by rote repetition or even test taking. Meaningful learning happens when people face a real-life challenge, need to find more information, and apply the information to solving the problem. Learning is reinforced when the information is relevant enough to help them solve more problems down the road.

If we want math concepts to stick and our kids to actually remember and use them throughout their lives, we need to challenge them with projects they personally want to accomplish. For example:

- using fractions in a recipe while making cookies they actually get to eat
- using statistics to decide their chance of winning a favorite game
- budgeting for a field trip
- designing and measuring the parts for building a reading nook in the classroom
- figuring out the costs involved in caring for different class pets

Students become the ones seeking the lessons and craving the math skills needed to achieve goals they actually care about.

Coding: Math's Gateway Drug

Computer programs are terrific tools for teaching these concepts in meaningful ways and helping numbers-averse students realize they're actually "good at math." Some of the most basic programs simply move objects on a screen based on simple mathematical instructions. For instance, students use basic math and geometry to tell a sprite to move forward one space, right one degree, and then repeat 359 times in order to draw a circle.

As students gain confidence and familiarity with math tools, they can begin building more complex solutions to more advanced problems. They may discover complicated math formulas can function as computer code. For example, have your students plug this code into a Google search bar and see what happens.[2]

sqrt(cos(x))cos(300x)+sqrt(abs(x))-0.7)(4-x*x)^0.01,
sqrt(6-x^2), -sqrt(6-x^2) from -4.5 to 4.5

As they test and explore this code and others, they get much more interested in square roots, cosines, and algebra. Just wait until they realize grid points and polygons lead into the world of super-cool, 3D gaming graphics!

What's the importance of using code to make math relevant? The truth is everyone can love math—when it isn't presented as difficult and irrelevant. Help your students tell a new story by solving problems together, building on their past successes, and gaining confidence in their math skills along the way. Make those problems relevant with the help of coding.

Coding Is Fixing and Failure Is Fun

When teaching basic coding, failure comes fast and easy—and that's a good thing! Programs almost always fail to run the way our kids planned because computers can't read intentions! They follow instructions exactly, and humans almost never enter a perfect set of instructions on the first try.

> WHEN TEACHING BASIC CODING,
> FAILURE COMES FAST AND EASY—
> AND THAT'S A GOOD THING!

---

2 This code was originally posted to the do-it-yourself collaborative website *Instructables.com* by rocketman7.

When young coders run into a bug or an error they can't seem to solve, they often give up and say, "I'm not good at computer programming." But *all* computer programmers—from preteen amateurs to full-time professionals—experience bugs, errors, and frustrations *all* the time. In fact, encountering and fixing problems is almost entirely what they do!

Every time Kevin meets a computer programmer, he asks, "How much of your time is spent writing code compared to fixing broken code?" The answer is an 80/20 percentage split with the 80 percent focused on fixing code. Fixing failures *is* the work of a computer programmer. When your students are slogging through errors, tell them they're doing exactly what the coders of their favorite games, films, apps, and devices are doing right now!

Coding really is about careful thinking and constant debugging, making it a perfect medium for students to learn the problem-solving, testing, and persistence skills sought after by today's employers and entrepreneurs. The more we can help students anticipate and practice working through the feelings of despair when their code doesn't work, the more they'll develop the invaluable twenty-first century skill of *grit*.

However, even when we take the shame out of failure, students can still struggle to develop the persistence mindset of a successful computer coder, especially when they see other students succeeding faster. There's a large variation in how quickly different people take to coding, and this difference can quickly undermine the confidence of those who learn more slowly. Overcoming this is a critical mindset shift. Stress to these students how many different skill sets are involved in good computer programming, and how someone who learns a computer language's syntax quickly may struggle with visual design, effective data structuring, or truly user friendly interfaces. Assure your students that everyone goes through the same learning curve at their own pace.

Stumbling through the first rounds of getting a digital turtle to move around a screen is an explosion of learning. For example, students will learn

- the importance of *stop* and *repeat* functions,
- the critical nature of details in coding, and
- the underlying logical structure of giving explicit instructions to a computer.

Students learn these principles a little better with every failure—every time their turtle keeps walking right off the screen, or performs a 90-degree turn in the wrong spot, or they struggle to find a way to describe, step-by-step, how the turtle should perform a complicated task. Students will also discover none of these early "oops" does any harm or feels like failure the way a red X on a test sheet does. They just feel like fun challenges. In the end, students have a working program—tangible evidence of their persistence, creativity, and effort—built right on top of all those "failures."

As your students grow their skills, use higher-level tools, and get comfortable with failure as part of the learning experience, they'll naturally start using computer programs to solve real-life problems in school, at home, and in their community. For example, they might use a branching-tree logic app for choosing which extracurricular activities to join or a spreadsheet analyzing their classmates' music collections. Even students who don't continue coding after your class will know the value of working on a challenge all the way through and will have achieved *grit*.

Make Connections

Another great way to build intrinsic rewards into your coding lessons is to welcome non-programmers from the community into your classroom. Invite school alumni, family members, business leaders, and municipal workers to talk about how they use spreadsheets or specialized apps in their everyday lives and work. Maybe they even have a challenge your young coders could help solve! These role models can give students a sense of the widespread value of programming and the opportunities for jobs down the road for people with coding skills.

But don't stop with guest speakers. Take your students on field trips to see computer science in action. If you teach in a small town, visit a local computer repair shop or mobile wireless store. Connect with a tech-heavy company or college computing department. Medical facilities, financial institutions, and manufacturers all rely on cutting-edge computer and information technology today and may be great locations for a class visit.

Finally, connect your students with fellow learners across their region and around the world. Check out our Resources section to find educators and students around the world who want to collaborate on learning projects involving coding and computer science.

Fourth-Grade Inspiration

Fellow EdTechTeam community member Erica Armstrong shares what happened when her students got truly tech engaged.

My colleague, Tanya Hind, and I took a leap of faith to integrate coding into a major project for a class of fourth-grade students. This project combined science inquiry on habitats, learning coding through math, and integrating literacy through the creation of a game design document where students outlined their plans.

Using Scratch, each group created a fun-to-play game illustrating their understanding of the habitats they researched. In some games, animals searched for food sources while avoiding predators. Other games explored the impact of natural disasters or humans on habitats.

Our students blew us away with their accomplishments. Not only did they create great products—games more complex than we'd imagined—but the process was also so valuable to their learning. We were impressed by their persistence, problem-solving, and collaboration. They didn't rely on their teachers to be the experts; they took ownership of their learning by taking risks, finding similar games so they could study the code to pick up new skills, and sharing knowledge with one another. They were so proud of what they had created and felt they had really achieved something.

As Erica's story illustrates, our responsibility is to light within our students a steady flame of interest and confidence in technology and the skills it teaches. With the flame lit, we can step out of the way and let our students lead.

> OUR RESPONSIBILITY IS TO LIGHT WITHIN OUR STUDENTS A STEADY FLAME OF INTEREST AND CONFIDENCE IN TECHNOLOGY AND THE SKILLS IT TEACHES.

<6>

EARNING
ADMINISTRATORS' BUY-IN

L ike most of their teachers and students, the vast majority of school administrators don't know how to code. They don't have a deep understanding of computer science. And they don't know how to move students from texting and gaming to tech-ing and creating.

They may not even want to.

Technology by definition is a massive disruptor, changing our classroom interactions, our daily routines, our relationships, and how we teach at every level. And not all of those changes are good! We're all familiar with the frustration of our students (and colleagues) being distracted by glowing screens when we're trying to engage with them.

However, most educators we know have incredibly supportive administrations, eager to bring better technology education into the classroom. Our principals and district staff recognize computer science is really important for students. In fact, they're willing to serve as resources to help teachers who feel overwhelmed by other responsibilities, protecting their time so they can make coding lessons happen as well.

If you'd want your administration's support for a coding initiative in your class or school, make it easy for them to say *yes*. Compile a clear, affordable, achievable project proposal including the following elements:

- Goals, including intended learning outcomes
- Brief description of project
- Timeline
- Team members
- Any necessary supplies or administrative support
- Successful examples of models from other districts

Let's look at some of the common concerns you can address to keep administrators on your side.

> IF YOU'D WANT YOUR ADMINISTRATION'S SUPPORT FOR A CODING INITIATIVE IN YOUR CLASS OR SCHOOL, MAKE IT EASY FOR THEM TO SAY *YES*.

"Gotta Meet the Standards"

When it comes to our international obsession with standardized testing, teachers aren't the only ones who have it rough. School administrators know if students don't perform well on tests, entire districts will face serious consequences, up to and including a state takeover. So you'll have to demonstrate time spent coding won't hurt student performance on upcoming tests.

Fortunately, this is easy. We already know, with a little creativity, learning coding can actually improve test performance. (No—not by teaching kids to hack the testing software, as tempting as it may be!)

Refer to "Misconception #4: Coding doesn't fit the mandatory curriculum or standardized testing regimen" in Chapter 1. In short, computer science teaches general skills—logical thinking, making connections across lessons, data organization, persistence—to help with test taking. Lessons using coding can help students engage content more deeply and actively.

For instance, a fourth-grade class could use spreadsheets to sort and compare the *who, what, when, where,* and *why* of stories they've been reading. An eleventh grade history class could use animation software and mapping tools to show how a region's political boundaries changed over time. These approaches help students make connections across multiple lessons and topics, and increases the likelihood they'll remember the content for later testing.

Jared Amalong, who teaches in Placer County, California, shared this example:

> *Starting in 2008, I was fortunate to have administrators willing to give a county-wide computer science capstone course a try—and it was a success! Because of its applied nature, even students new to programming immersed themselves in the course and integrated their experience with other academic subjects. One former student, Bradley, extended his efforts in my course to his physics course, where he wrote many small programs to solve the challenging problems presented to him.*
>
> *In conversations with his parents and teachers, I learned Bradley's commitment to computer science renewed his commitment to his other academic studies. Bradley is now a computer science major in college and has begun applying his studies in an internship with LinkedIn. His story—like those of many other former students—demonstrates computer science is a model twenty-first century curricula as it prepared him for both college and career.*

"We Can't Afford It!"

Administrators' other biggest worry about coding in the classroom? Cost.

At some point, most schools have been burned by a bad investment in technology. Maybe the expensive classroom printers were always breaking down. Maybe the learning curve for shifting from Apples to PCs was too steep, and the district had to go back to Macs after a year or two. Maybe a costly mass purchase of tablets failed to deliver the promised education revolution. Negative tech history can lead administrators to slam the brakes on any project sounding remotely like a "tech fad."

Fortunately, this challenge is also easy to address. Start by calming your administrators' budgeting fears. Even if your school is flush with cash, learning computer science doesn't require new systems, special software, or expensive equipment. The school doesn't even need to provide computers! Explain basic coding lessons can involve chalk on the playground, branching-tree logic activities on paper, or board games built right in the classroom.

One of Kevin's favorite letters to send home asks families for their old, discarded Android phones, which students then use to create and test their own apps. These are terrific tools for learning real-world coding. You could request used electronic children's toys, out-of-date video game consoles, or ask around the district for computers and electronics no longer in service. No new dollars are required.

When students are ready to learn more advanced skills, free and low-cost options abound. Introductory coding devices cost a fraction of the price of a new computer fleet. Very simple computers, such as the popular programming learning device Raspberry Pi kit (about $30), and highly functional yet streamlined ones, such as Google's Chromebook (about $200), keep the costs to a bare minimum while allowing students to explore an infinite range of coding opportunities.

< What Is A Raspberry Pi? >

The Raspberry Pi is a low-cost, credit-card-sized computer that plugs into a computer monitor or television, and uses a standard keyboard and mouse. It is a capable little device that enables people of all ages to explore computing, and to learn how to program in languages like Scratch and Python. It's capable of doing everything you'd expect a desktop computer to do, from browsing the Internet and playing high-definition video, to making spreadsheets, word-processing, and playing games.

What's more, the Raspberry Pi has the ability to interact with the outside world, and has been used in a wide array of digital maker projects, from music machines and parent detectors to weather stations and tweeting birdhouses with infrared cameras. We want to see the Raspberry Pi being used by kids all over the world to learn to program and understand how computers work.

—RaspberryPi.org[1]

Finally, administrators may hesitate to invest in or support a project they aren't absolutely sure will work. In this case, keep your proposals small, simple, and discreet. Pitch your ideas for EdTech initiatives as "tests" and "pilots" rather than ongoing programs. Build up some wins and smaller successes. Share inspiring examples from others schools and help connect your administrators with the educational technology community, giving them the opportunity to see coding used in the classroom in awesome ways.

---

1 *What is a Raspberry Pi?* Raspberry Pi Foundation, March 26, 2014, Video, 1:43 minutes. Retrieved from *raspberrypi.org/help/what-is-a-raspberry-pi*

< What Is A Chromebook? >

Chromebooks are laptops running Google's Chrome OS rather than Windows, Mac OS X, Linux, or other operating systems. Almost everything done on a Chromebook is done online through the Google Chrome web browser and web-based apps. Chromebooks come with multiple gigabytes of free, cloud-based storage for documents and other files, and music files can be stored to the laptop's hard drive.

For times when an Internet connection isn't available, Google offers plenty of offline services allowing you to write and read emails, explore and edit files in Google Drive Online, check your calendar, take notes, and read web pages you've saved in advance.

Chromebooks have taken off because of their low cost, ease of use, and strong battery life. They're a terrific tool for day-to-day use. However, Chromebooks aren't designed for intensive 3D game play, video processing, or installation-required programs such as Photoshop and Skype. But web-friendly alternatives such as GIMP and Google Hangouts abound, and web-based versions of popular software are showing up everywhere. For instance, scaled-down versions of Microsoft Office Suite programs are available through the free, cloud-based Microsoft Online service.

Spreading the Word

Want to really blow your administrators' minds? Computer and information science is in such high demand, with impacts in so many fields, introducing a coding program to a school practically guarantees strong outside support. Share examples in your proposal of coding projects in other schools that inspired more community engagement or donations. Once you've initiated a program, make a plan to share the results with the circles of support around your school.

Families and Alumni

Starting with parents, grandparents, and alumni is a great way to build enthusiasm for your vision. These people are already invested in your school community—or at least in the children who will benefit from the project. Welcome them to be part of the coding push! Hold open houses and show-and-tell nights for families. Invite them to come learn and grow their own skills at evening and weekend workbench sessions, or share their expertise by speaking to your classes or after-school clubs. And definitely encourage them to spread the word about the project with their colleagues and communities!

Social Media

Sharing the word through posts to your school's Facebook page is great, but don't be afraid to think bigger. Help your students put together videos documenting their projects (and their needs). Offer instructional videos and websites explaining the same topics your students are learning. Consider a crowdfunding effort using sites like Kickstarter and GoFundMe. Connect your classrooms and colleagues with groups around the world to help your projects grow.

Local Media

Local newspapers, popular blogs, radio stations, and television news stations can help spread the word about your efforts and attract community support. Let the positive publicity around EdTech initiatives ripple out to your entire school district and its leaders.

Local Business and Nonprofit Networks

Companies and small businesses have supported local schools as long as schools have been around. They know investments made in a community's children today will pay off with a stronger workforce and paying customers in the future. But thanks to the Internet, this support (and more) can come from far outside a school's local community. Look at what has changed in the Internet age:

- Today *every* school has access to wealthy business and nonprofit networks. Those connections no longer depend on a school's immediate neighborhood. We now have the tools to bridge geography (for far-flung rural schools), politics (for schools in struggling or war-torn regions), and socioeconomics (for children growing up in low-income areas).

- Our students are in the remarkable position of being able to *partner* with their sponsors, not just accept assistance and hopefully emerge ten or twenty years from now as productive customers, staff, and citizens. As students engage with technology, they provide helpful information about their community's needs, preferences, and skills. Older students can engage directly with nonprofit groups, using their research, coding, and computer science skills to help with local projects.

- Businesses and nonprofits now have unlimited ways to help schools. In addition to donating money and equipment, or providing a guest speaker once a year, they can easily share data for class projects, offer live virtual tours of their facilities, or collaborate with a school community on a major real-world problem. They can offer internships, mentoring, and professional recommendations from thousands of miles away.

Some organizations may be more willing to respond when they learn about the positive effects technology learning has on your students, particularly female students and those from underprivileged backgrounds. Highlight how coding opportunities can help some of our most disadvantaged children break the generational cycle of poverty and transform their entire region's business climate. By getting involved with your students' technology projects, businesses and non-profits can create a healthier, more productive community in the very near future.

Get to the Launch Pad

Okay, so you've addressed the biggest concerns an administrator might have about welcoming educational technology into your classroom. What happens if you're still faced with major resistance? In the immortal words of U.S. Navy Rear Admiral Grace Hopper, a computer programming pioneer, "It's easier to ask forgiveness than it is to get permission." Don't challenge any direct orders, of course. But you might try the following approaches:

- Find some small "guerrilla projects" to launch in your classroom.
- Collaborate with fellow instructors and community leaders to work technology into your lessons without incurring major costs in time or money.
- Create a coding adventure event, camp, or after-school program outside the official school purview.
- Connect with education technology experts and consultants for ideas on shifting the culture while helping your students thrive.

When an entire school community gets behind an educational technology initiative, amazing things can happen. Together, classrooms and administrators alike can reach out to the community and foster powerful partnerships to help our students truly thrive.

Like all such projects, however, it takes good communication and a lot of groundwork. We'll tell you the same thing we tell our students: Be persistent! Your students' futures are worth the effort.

<7>

BUILD YOUR EXPERTISE

 ### *Kevin's Classroom*

After my first experimental forays into teaching technology, I was hungry to learn and share more. I wanted my students future-ready, poised for twenty-first century success. I was totally convinced technology education was the key to achieving those goals, but I didn't want to change my career and spend ten years getting a degree in programming.

Thank goodness for the 2010 Google for Education summit. This extremely valuable program introduced me to people from all over the world who were creating amazing educational technology experiences—none of them with specialized computer science degrees. I saw how regional support groups and online communities enabled these educators to stay on top of educational technology.

This first experience led me to years of discovering new tools based on others' recommendations. After exploring them in my classroom, I passed them on to others. I'm still not a true computer programmer (and probably never will be), but I'm an expert at getting my students fired up to learn.

As we educators share ideas, play with tools, and experiment together, we learn. So rest assured, you don't have to earn a degree in computer science, take a side job as a coder, or attend every hot new tech conference to inspire your students and incorporate code. You just need to teach core computer science skills students can draw from, no matter what devices they use or careers they pursue.

What to Learn

Technology evolves rapidly. Today's hot new programming languages and revolutionary devices will be antiquated by the time our kids submit their first résumés. Since no one knows what tech is going to look like down the road, we teach basic coding. No matter what coding language they learn, students will be familiar with principles to help them develop logical, step-by-step thinking, creative problem-solving skills, persistence, and collaboration. Those building blocks let them adapt to any tech they encounter in the future. As such, a programming-friendly teacher should do two things:

1. Stay familiar with current events in education and technology.
2. Work to understand the underlying principles and practices of coding, which drive every electronic device in the world.

Staying involved in communities of technology educators will keep you familiar with current events. To help you begin to understand coding, we'll cover the following:

- computer languages and why they matter
- how to incorporate code into your lessons
- resources for furthering your learning and creating more in-depth lessons

Pick some of the lessons from in this book, open your laptop, and play around. Prepare to be empowered! The world of electronics will never look quite the same way again.

What Is a Computer Language?

A computer language is a system of delivering instructions and data for machines to act on. This language—or program—is the actual code telling our devices what to do, whether it's to print a document, power a website server, or run the International Space Station. To convey its instructions to the devices, the language has to be simple enough to translate into the physical world of the machine. As such, messages are sent using one of the simplest pieces of information: a *binary* signal.

Bi·na·ry ('bīnərē)

1. *(adjective)* Something having two parts
2. *(noun)* A system of numerical notation with two elements: 0 or 1

In the human world, binary messages take many forms. A finger tap, bell toll, or drum beat has two parts: sound or no sound. A lantern can be covered or uncovered. Morse code is a form of binary: dit or dah. In electronic devices, binary information takes the form of an electrical impulse or magnetic fluctuation. If an electronic switch is open and electricity is moving through, it's considered ON. If the switch is closed, the message is OFF. Information delivered!

The most famous form of binary messaging is binary code: 1/0 (one / zero). Binary code tells an electronic chip switch to open (ON) with a 1 and close (OFF) with a 0. Abstract information takes physical form in this way. Regardless of what programming language you use, it eventually translates your instructions down to the physical level of the machine in ones and zeros. For this reason, binary is sometimes known as "machine code."

Want to make your budding computer programmers laugh? Post this in your classroom:

"There are only 10 kinds of people in the world: those who understand binary, and those who don't."

So how do we get from 1/0 to the Internet? String these 1/0 "bits" (binary digits) of information together, and you have binary code:

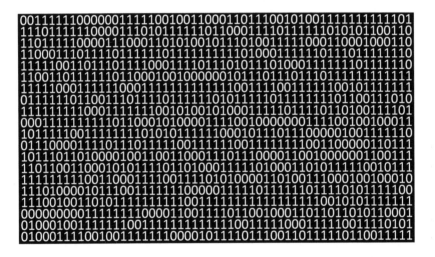

These strings of ones and zeroes are the foundational instructions telling nearly all modern devices—from computers to medical scanners to compact disc players to smartphones—how to operate.

< How Many "Words" —————
in a Binary Language? >

Just as we combine letters to form words to represent ideas, programming languages combine 1/0 bits to form strings to represent information. For instance, a one-bit binary string can convey either of two pieces of information: zero or one.

0

1

A two-bit binary string can have four different arrangements, meaning it can convey four pieces of information:

00

10 01

11

Add another bit to form a three-bit series, and the options double again.

000

001 010 100

011 101 110

111

A four-bit binary string offers sixteen potential pieces of information:

0000

0001 0010 0100 1000

0011 0101 0110 1001 1010 1100

0111 1011 1101 1110

1111

And so on.

The most popular binary languages today use an 8-bit system, allowing up to *256* unique combinations. An 8-bit string is called a *byte*. But even longer binary codes exist—with 16-bit strings, 32-bit strings, and even variable-bit strings combining the best of multiple binary code systems. When combined, those incredibly simple ones and zeroes can deliver a nearly infinite amount of information.

For a terrific description of how binary works, check out *computer.howstuffworks.com/bytes.htm.*

To us, these strings of ones and zeroes look like a chaotic series of hundreds of random numbers; but to a machine, they are incredibly clear instructions. Depending on the binary code system it's using, the machine will convert the list of numbers into individual strings.

Here's where things get interesting. Just as the word *pan* translates as *cooking tool* in English, *bread* in Spanish, and *Bang!* in French, a binary code string translates as different items—letters, numbers, symbols, sounds, pixel colors, etc.—depending on which computer language is being used. For instance, the eight-bit series 01101010 can be translated in different computer languages as:

- the letter *j*
- the decimal number 106
- the hexadecimal code 6a
- the Ascii85 code C&
- the Base32 code NI
- and so on...

In the same way we combine words to share millions of ideas, programmers combine binary strings to share millions of instructions and data points.

Beyond Binary

Today's coders almost never work at the level of binary machine languages, though. They work with higher-level programming languages, invented to convert millions of machine-level instructions into a single higher-level command.

< Computer Language Family Tree >

Machine-Level

With very few exceptions, all machines "read" instructions in binary code, a purely mathematical language. The strings of binary are sometimes written in octal, decimal, hexadecimal, and other versions of code more friendly to human eyes. However, these are simply different ways of labeling the binary ones and zeroes the machine responds to.

Assembly Languages

Slightly higher up the evolutionary tree of programming are simple assembly languages. These use words (ADD, START) rather than numbers (01101110, 11010110), but are still incredibly basic instructions with barely a single translation step between the programmer and the machine.

Machine codes are specific to the devices they were designed for (e.g., a Nikon digital camera uses a different machine code than a Canon). Assembly languages, as cleaned-up versions of machine code, are machine-specific as well.

Third Generation / High-Level Languages

Third generation (3GL) or high-level languages emerged in the 1950s and were the first to use abstract code and formal syntax, including variables, loops, objects, and Boolean logic. These languages—COBOL and FORTRAN, C++ and Java—are more user-friendly and automatically perform some of the background operations such as memory management.

They must be translated back down to machine code by compilers in order for devices to perform their instructions. While this adds an additional layer of programming, it frees up the coding so it can apply to more than one particular type of machine.

Fourth-Generation Languages

Developed in the 1970s, 80s, and 90s, these languages overlap with 3GL to provide even more user-friendly experiences. They tend to work with large amounts of information at once and involve libraries of pre-coded instructions. Examples include Python, Ruby, SQL, and Unix Shell.

Visual Programming Languages

Any programming language using graphics instead of text to communicate instructions is a visual language. These are the most commonly used languages in the educational realm and include the block-based coding languages familiar to users of *Code.org* (Blockly), MIT's learning platform (Scratch), and the Hopscotch learning app (Hopscotch).

Other visual programming tools combine drag-and-drop icons with flowchart-style diagramming. These are used for professional purposes by musicians, game designers, data system managers, simulators, business data analysts, and many other types of developers.

In the 1950s, FORTRAN and COBOL were created as some of the earliest "high-level" languages. Their data and instructions were entered into computer systems using hundreds of punch cards kept in precise order—a time-consuming process. If a change was needed, new cards had to be created and old ones replaced. And pity the programmer who dropped a box of cards causing entire programs to fall out of order!

In the 1960s, as computer processing speeds grew, programs could be keyed directly into computer terminals, making the data much easier to edit and interact with. By the 1970s, personal computers and arcade games emerged, offering programs regular people could use without performing any coding themselves.

Over the past half century, as processing power exploded, thousands of programming languages were created. Some were designed for a single unique machine to perform just a few basic tasks—similar to a handheld calculator performing only addition, subtraction, multiplication, and division. Others were created to be used by millions of devices worldwide to accomplish a massive range of tasks, and are many steps away from the core binary code.

Each language is designed for a different purpose and has its own benefits and drawbacks. Some work better for web page development, others for mobile applications. Some are preferable for real-time video communications, some for CGI effects in movies, and so on.

Some of the easiest languages to use are block-based codes, highly visual tools for delivering instructions. They're used by the most popular coding education sites today, which model core concepts such as logical order, loops, and variables. These principles of coding apply no matter what language students move on to use.

Here's a quick overview of some of today's major programming languages and what they're commonly used for.

To build an attractive, interactive website: **HTML, CSS**

To create web applications: **Ruby on Rails**, or **PHP**

To process data or explore databases: **SQL** or **Python**

To make a game or online app: **JavaScript**

To learn pro-level game and software development: **C++**

To develop mobile apps: **iOS** for Apple products, **Java** for Android

If you want to move beyond block-based languages to teach real-world code, spend time experimenting with a variety of popular languages. Then pick one of the major languages and go from there. Kevin, for instance, has become interested in Python, which he uses to code on Raspberry Pi. Ria, who learned the basics of HTML when building websites in college, is exploring CSS. But the particular platform is less important than exposure to the concepts all these languages teach.

No matter which one your students learn, they'll pick up syntax and structure which translates easily to the others. In fact, many companies are willing to hire coders who don't know the particular language they use, as long as the coders have experience and foundational knowledge in others. To give you an idea of how valuable language experience can be for our students, here's where the jobs are as of 2016, according to CodeDojo.org:

- **SQL** (pronounced "sequel") provides roughly 50,000 jobs for coders.
- **Java** and **JavaScript**, which share a name but are very different languages, are both in the 40,000 jobs range.
- **C#** (pronounced "C-sharp") came in next at roughly 25,000 jobs.
- **Python, C++** ("C plus plus"), **PHP, iOS**, and **Ruby on Rails** range from 15,000 to 5,000 jobs each.
- Watch for growing use of Apple's 2014 programming language, **iOS/Swift!**

Languages of the Future

What does the future of programming languages hold? Certainly there will be more of them, as processing speeds expand and new devices are developed. As a recent article in *WIRED Magazine* proclaimed, our most advanced devices will soon be trained, not programmed. Some machines are already designed to follow logical procedures to come up with their own solutions to problems. Essentially these machines are programmed to use true artificial intelligence!

Meanwhile, researchers are exploring ways to develop new, more powerful versions of machine code, replacing binary code with ternary, quaternary, quinary, and beyond. Then there's the theory of quantum computing. This replaces the ones and zeros of binary code with quantum bits, or qubits, and allows programmers to use the quantum phenomena of entanglement (two "bits" maintain an identical state, no matter how far apart they are) and superposition (a single bit can exist in multiple states, such as one and zero, at once).

Clearly, the future of computing is beyond imagining.

Core Concepts

Daily personal and business computer programming, however, is still a human responsibility. We need young people trained in coding to program our coffee makers, traffic analyzers, social media algorithms, and cost analysis spreadsheets—not to mention our self-driving vehicles, solar panel grid integration, pandemic virus response, and trips to Mars! So let's get up to speed on four of the core principles these young coders will need to know.

Syntax

Having previously taught English, we know it is a pretty challenging language, even for native speakers. English is a centuries-old language borrowing sounds, words, sentence structure, idioms, and even grammatical rules from many other languages—and often mangles them in the process. People are easily confused by homonyms like *their* and *they're*, or write *the Jones's* when they meant *the Joneses* or even *the Jones'*. And professional grammarians are still arguing about the Oxford comma!

Of course, if you misspell a word in English, use the wrong punctuation, or just place words in a strange order, you might get a laugh, but you'll generally still be understood. Just look at most text message conversations! In fact, you might even create a new addition to the language. However, this simply isn't the situation when it comes to computer languages. Depending on what language is used, the *syntax*—the set of rules defining how each character entered in a command line will be interpreted—is absolutely fixed.

In HTML, for instance, the syntax requires all commands be enclosed in angle brackets. Each command applies to all following text until the same command is applied with a forward slash in front of it, canceling the earlier effect:

- \<b\>**text enclosed by these commands will be bold**\</b\> but not text that follows.
- \<i\>*text enclosed by these commands will be italicized*\</i\> but not text that follows.
- \<a href="http://codeineveryclass.com"\><u>text enclosed by these commands will hyperlink to the specified website</u>\</a\> but not text that follows.

When you use the language correctly, the computer will always interpret and act on it in exactly the same way. While good for troubleshooting, this also means the language is totally unforgiving. If you fail to place a forward slash in front of a canceling command in HTML, the original effect will continue throughout the entire page. Misplace a curly bracket in C++, fail to place a semicolon at the end of an instruction line in JavaScript, or misspell "print" in Python, and the same thing happens: an error! Fortunately, just as most word processors and social media sites have spellcheckers today, you can download syntax checkers to help you catch programming mistakes before they trigger an error.

Syntax is unique to each computer language, although languages often share elements in common. Once you've figured out how a language's syntax works, you can use it to program any number of ideas into reality.

Variables

Variables are changeable elements in a set of instructions. When the variable changes, so does the outcome. Most of our experience with variables is in the realm of math—algebra to be exact. For example, $3 + x = \underline{\ \ }$. The solution to the problem depends on the value of x.

If $x = 5$, then the solution is 8. If $x = 7$, the solution is 10. The same thing applies to computer programming, but we apply many different kinds of values to the variables.

Let's say we create a very simple computer program to greet users. Instead of "x," we create a variable called "firstname." Whatever is entered in this variable field will appear as part of the outcome of the program: "Hello + *variable_firstname* = output." When a user runs the program, the computer will print out a string including the value entered for the user's first name: "Hello Jayden" or "Hello Brie" or "Hello Nyana," and so on.

This process becomes very useful in designing programs involving user input. Using this concept, you can customize programs for each user to make them more personalized, interactive, and engaging.

Control Structure

A control structure is a set of instructions telling an electronic device what to do when a change happens. A digital alarm, for instance, will turn the alarm tone ON when the time changes to match what the control structure is waiting for. Control structures usually follow Boolean logic principles which use conditional statements such as IF – THEN. Combining logic and variables, the control structure code for the digital alarm looks like this:

> IF
> *variable* time = 0615
> THEN
> *run* alarm

The actual terms and symbols used to deliver those instructions will vary based on the computer language being used, but the underlying ideas will be the same.

Here's another example, dropping in the Boolean AND (which requires more than one variable to be true before a change will trigger) and ELSE (which provides a different action if one or both variables are false).

A common use of this language is seen each time you log in to your personal email account. When you reach the login page, you see a prompt to enter two variables: your username and your password. The code behind the scene may look like this:

IF

variable username = WorldsBestTeacher

AND

IF

variable password = Deserves1Apple

THEN

run open email window

ELSE

run "Incorrect username or password"

Repetition

Some people say the entire purpose of a computer is to perform repetitive tasks faster and more accurately than a human can, and this idea is built right into the code itself. Most coding languages include commands causing machines to perform certain actions over and over and over again. For instance, a drawing program could be instructed to draw a ten-pixel line, make a ninety-degree turn to the right, and repeat both actions three times, making drawing a square faster and easier for the programmer.

One basic control structure used for repetition is the *loop*, which starts an action and repeats it until a particular instruction is complete. Loops come in several forms, including the WHILE structure. Going back to our alarm clock, you can use WHILE and the clock's ON/OFF switch to make it to stop sounding:

WHILE

variable alarm = ON

run = alarm

Once the variable is set to OFF, the WHILE loop will end.

Data Structure

Data structures simplify the process of saving and organizing data. Lists, categories, trees, heaps, graphs, arrays—all of these are different ways of sorting, storing, and displaying data. Besides saving time for coders, these structures help us think about the information we process in our education, work, and daily lives. When we teach our students the different methods for ordering and categorizing information, our students discover all kinds of new possibilities for interacting with the data of their lives. They boost their skills in abstract thinking, creativity, logic, and problem-solving.

Where to Learn More

If you're interested in gaining more knowledge of the theory of coding, check out the self-directed courses on languages and applications listed in the Resources section. These sites provide plenty of basic information and practice to help you develop your programming wizardry. But sometimes it's helpful to go offline and use some old-school approaches to deepen your learning. So we've listed some of our favorite foundational technology books for laypeople and educational technology guides in the Resources section as well.

We also highly recommend face-to-face learning relationships. While these can take many forms, a programming class at a local community college or other center is an ideal opportunity to get both expert advice and practice in a learning environment similar to the ones your students experience. As coding grows in popularity, meet-up groups of local programmers and learners are appearing in cities all over the country. Tap into these, as well as local professional organizations, to find not only opportunities to learn and practice your skills, but also to discover valuable contacts for class projects and after-school programs. As an educator, your perspective is important and can inspire programmers to develop better tools and community leadership for the coming generations of coders.

Finally, nothing beats good old-fashioned hands-on learning. Take out your laptop, open a programming website, plug in some code, and play!

Beyond the Lessons

Learning to program is not a finite task. Not only will there always be more to discover about computer programming, there will always be people who know more about a specific coding language than you do. The nature of coding is collaborative; we have to use each other as resources.

Once you've established a basic level of coding understanding, you'll have a better sense of its possibilities, equipping you to explain code to kids and to solve all kinds of problems in your classroom and career field. You'll also have the foundational understanding you need to effectively communicate with experts who can help you accomplish the tasks you envision. In fact, those experts just might include your own students!

Above all, keep practicing the skills you've learned. Just a couple of hours every month will build your skills and mold you into a successful programming educator in just a few short years.

<8>

How to Launch a Coding Program

Congratulations! If you've been reading straight through the book, you've come to understand how valuable coding skills are for every student. You've learned how to build support at every level for computer programming in your classroom, from students and colleagues to administrators and the community. You've even learned a little about coding, yourself.

Now you're ready to launch. So how do you take a classroom of computer programming newbies and turn them into future-ready students? Launching a coding program is like launching any other project:

- Create a plan with clear, achievable, measurable goals.
- Draft a timeline made up of small activities building toward the goal.
- Remember a mantra Kevin first saw on a poster in the offices of Facebook: "Done is better than perfect."

Step 1: Start Small

To reach your goal, no matter how lofty, we recommend starting small. Adding coding instruction in to your classroom doesn't require completely transforming your curriculum. Take one lesson you currently teach and find a way to bring coding into it. Check out the next chapter or our Resources section for ideas.

Test your lesson. What kinds of responses did you get? What was challenging? What did your students learn? What did *you* learn? Based on what you learn, look for more educational technology that would be simple and relevant to your students.

"Rinse and repeat" with more lessons, getting a feel for what works and doesn't work in your classroom. Lessons should clearly and easily tie in with your curriculum and the resources you already have available. Make sure to document your process and share what you've learned.

In general, beginner coders all have the same core lessons to learn:

- How to break a task down into step-by-step instructions
- How to communicate instructions in ways a computer can follow
- How to troubleshoot to get the desired results

As students develop their basic coding skills, you can advance to more complex exercises, using coding technology for

- creative problem-solving,
- project-based learning,
- lessons in computer theory (the history and scope of programming languages and technology), and
- lessons building subject knowledge and expertise in your class's academic curriculum.

To help students build proficiency with a specific program or skill, find out what they already know. Depending on the access they've had to technology, your kids will have different comfort levels related to learning coding. Differentiate your lessons to meet both beginner and advanced students' needs. Set up your lesson plan so those who finish quickly can help others. Let students work in teams to practice more advanced skills themselves.

Step 2: Set the Stage

If your project involves devices, computers, Internet connections, or other technology, make sure things are set up to run smoothly. Have backup plans for the inevitable crashes, website issues, and Internet outages—or have your students generate their own!

Outside of class instruction time, scatter "bread crumbs" for your students to follow. Put up posters of famous computer scientists. Bring books about fun programming projects. Post lists of introductory websites such as *Code.org* and *GetHopscotch.com* and invite students to spend time exploring coding outside class for extra credit.

No matter the level at which they're working, it's important to create a safe space for kids to learn and fail. Remind students often that perfection leads to paralysis. After every exercise, publicly name and celebrate the disappointments and shortfalls, along with the persistence and tools your students used to eventually solve their challenges.

Step 3: Bring in the Booster Rockets

Start gathering support. Share what you've been trying and learning with colleagues, students' families, and learning communities, such as those listed at the back of this book. Educate your community. Help them understand the value, relevance, and ease of introducing students to coding and computer science. Share examples from successful efforts at other schools. Remember those supportive online EdTech networks; they come in handy!

Whether you're looking for ideas on classroom management, project resources, or community presentations, conversation with fellow tech educators is invaluable. Don't forget to share your own experiences and ideas. We encourage all teachers to dive into these social networks to learn from colleagues around the world. Visit the Resources list at the back of this book to connect with global educational technology communities for additional ideas and collaboration opportunities.

Step 4: Start Growing

Once you've found success with basic lessons in computer science and built a community of support, it's time to go deeper. Work with your students to find some larger, longer-term goals and projects to pursue. You could:

- develop an app to help organize class schedules and responsibilities
- design a branching-logic system to identify and protect plants and wildlife around the school
- convince community leaders to support after-school busing by presenting a spreadsheet analysis of student data
- build a robot to compete in regional and state robotics events

Find ways the project can help meet your curriculum requirements. If you get stuck, ask your educational technology community.

Once goals are in place, help students identify what they'll need to achieve them. If a project requires new devices or supplies, let your class strategize about how to get them. Will they obtain used devices from families? Hold a fundraiser at the school? Launch a Kickstarter campaign? What can they create a workaround for?

Have them do the same with expertise. Will they learn what they need through trial and error? Websites and videos? Books? Field trips? Bringing in professional coders or data analysts?

Step 5: Time to Play!

Fun projects are the best! Computer programming and data sciences call for a tremendous amount of persistence and imagination. Our kids have what it takes—watch them hunting on Pokémon Go—but they have to believe the experience is worthwhile. Twenty-first century traits get killed when students feel they're doing meaningless drudgery or they're caught up in perfectionism, worried they have to "do it right."

Coach your students to view everything they're working on as an experiment, an exploration, and a learning opportunity on the way to *their* goal. If they are working on their own goals, they will be motivated from within, by curiosity and inner drive rather than stress or fear.

Step 6: More Than a Grade

Along the same lines, give your classes opportunities to celebrate their accomplishments. For most students, receiving recognition for their work is a great celebration. Recognition can be as simple as students posting their work online to a shared classroom folder or giving a report to a small group. Or you can help them go big and experience pageantry—a true rite of passage. How big? Capstone projects can be delivered in an on-stage event, open to the school, families, and the larger community. They could even be filmed and broadcast online to learning communities around the world.

More importantly, help students learn performance isn't the only path for celebration. Coach them to celebrate the larger meaning in their accomplishments:

- Whose lives have been touched by their work?
- What are they contributing to the world through what they learned and created for this project?
- How are they using their powers for good?

We've seen how motivating this kind of meaningful, project-oriented, highly public work can be. The year-long "20time" capstone projects Kevin introduced at York School (*20time.org*) have spread to hundreds of other schools worldwide and created a movement. Collaborative, long-term projects are a perfect fit for students learning to code.

One of the best tools for solidifying learning from a project is a final presentation. This could be as simple as showing classmates a replay of an animated turtle they coded to walk a path in the shape of a square, or filming their robot's first steps and sharing it on YouTube. Or it could be as complicated as having students give a live presentation to the entire school community demonstrating a year-long effort to develop an anti-bullying app.

Giving young learners the opportunity to share their achievements in a public and meaningful way is important because it helps them to learn to identify what's valuable about their work, recognize their own capabilities, and experience the empowerment of achieving a vision. Final presentations also give them the experience of completing a big task—no small gift in today's world of "always more."

Beyond the Basics

While teaching students how to program a computer from the ground up is deeply beneficial, it's only one of the ways you can inspire your classes to become advanced technology users. Here are some others to consider:

- Go beyond *how to use a search engine* or *let's write a paper online*! Expose kids to professional software—computer animation tools, 3D printing, satellite mapping, medical technologies, etc.—and its uses. Even if all you can do is read about these resources, make sure your students know what's available and what's possible, and help them dream of even more.
- Share profiles and stories of people using technology to change the world through creating digital graphics for major films, saving the environment, bringing the Internet to remote villages, rescuing people from disasters, and so on.
- Connect students with people, places, and information around the world using video chat, virtual tours, and database exploration.

- Lead students in projects making a direct difference in their lives, and help them use technology to boost their work. Guide them to use coding, devices, and computational thinking to produce and spread their work and their message.

Those are just a few ways you can encourage students to explore the valuable skills related to different programming languages, technology design, and tech-based problem-solving. The common theme to all of them? Shifting students from being technology consumers to content creators, able to use their tech for good. Teach them technology is an unprecedented tool for giving them more say in their lives, stronger voices in their communities, and more power over what happens to them and their world. Then give them experiences to prepare them for real impact in the future, both in their personal careers and in the wider community.

Doing this not only launches a coding program—it builds a more empowered world.

<9>
Coding Lessons

I t's time to put all this learning into practice! Let's dive into some lessons that you can incorporate into your classroom, whether you're teaching kindergartners or high school seniors, math geeks, music nuts, young poets, science lovers, or history buffs. (You might want to grab a computer and test some of the lessons as you read.)

How to Use This Chapter

Each lesson appears with stated goals, a step-by-step description, and necessary resources. Many of these lessons were submitted from EdTechTeam's social networks, including Twitter and Google+. We've tweaked the lessons and included these awesome educators' names with the projects they suggested. We invite you to join the forum to discover more about what these teachers are doing in their classrooms.

The lessons that follow are grouped by basic coding skill and type—pseudocode, block-based, branching logic, etc.—*not* by traditional school subject or grade level because most tech lessons can work well for multiple subjects. For example, an app serving as a restaurant tip calculator can qualify as both math training and a lesson in social studies. Developing a music program to set different electronic instruments to play the same tones helps students explore principles of science as well as music.

< Our "No-Silos" Soapbox >

The world doesn't work in silos. Grocery stores, professional sports teams, or wildlife parks—every business is a tech industry now. Everything requires excellent communication, reasoning, and analysis skills, and every career requires a healthy understanding of finance, math, and an ability to use spreadsheets and statistics. We should approach education in the classroom in the same way.

We believe in integrating curriculum. While it's important to have expert teachers and instruction in all subjects, we find project-based learning is far more effective for student retention of instruction in meaningful ways. Academic content—whether it is geometry or English or physical education—works best when integrated into larger, personally relevant projects, rather than locked into a series of unrelated forty-five-minute classes.

After all, integration is how people of all ages learn in the real world. They take on projects for their jobs, their homes, and their communities, only to discover they have to learn something in order to finish the work. Not only are they motivated at that point to learn the content, they're far more likely to remember and use their knowledge in the future.

For generations, most schools haven't let students learn in this natural, empowering way. We strongly believe that our educational system needs to fundamentally change for our children to grow up with a chance to thrive in the twenty-first century. Bringing high-quality computer skills into your class is an important step toward making this vision a reality.

The same holds true for grade levels. A beginner project can be just as entertaining for a high school senior as it is for a kindergartner. The goals for beginner coders are the same at any age: build familiarity and confidence with technology and computer programming while developing fundamental skills in logic, analysis, and troubleshooting.

So consider this a permission slip to deviate from the script. Play with the ideas! Use the lessons—not as instructions set in stone, but as inspiration for what could be possible when coding comes into your classroom. Find ways to use each lesson to help your students explore the academic curriculum. Scale lessons up or down as appropriate for your students' ages and expertise. Let students riff off the basic lessons personally and adapt them to meet their needs.

When you're ready, share your ideas for tweaks to the lessons and post your entirely new lessons too! Use Twitter with the hashtag *#codeineveryclass*, or go to the EdTechTeam Global Community at *community.codeineveryclass.org*.

Pseudocode

Pseudocode is any activity using step-by-step instructions *not* involving a computer. The Playground Coder exercise from Chapter 4, where students draw a chalk grid on the playground and give a "robot" student instructions for moving and acting, is pseudocode.

Pseudocode is helpful for both beginners and more advanced coders. For beginners, it's an easy and safe introduction to the world of computing. Pseudocode helps more experienced coders relate the concepts of computing to the real world and better understand the value of what they're learning.

If your pseudocode activity involves translating real-world instructions into a programming language, you can either use the existing structure of a language your class is learning or make up a code of your own. As long as your made-up code is logical and precise, it will work!

Coder Says

THE GOAL

Using whole-body learning and play, students practice breaking tasks into logical instructions.

THE LESSON

This is the coding version of Simon Says. Of course, "Simon" is replaced by "Coder," and the players are "Computers" instead of followers.

Give instructions students have to follow, but use coding terminology. For example, if the Coder says, "Left bracket, jump right," the players should all jump right. However, if the Coder says, "Jump right," (omitting the coding term "Left bracket") any student who jumps is out!

As students learn more coding, you can add more layers to the instructions. Instead of the coder giving a single instruction at a time, a list of instructions could be given. If the instructions are given in correct order, students follow them and their task is accomplished. If the Coder gives them in an invalid order, the "Computers" shouldn't follow them! If the students do follow an incorrect order, have them figure out why it was incorrect before moving on.

Code the Classroom

THE GOAL

Students recognize and apply the principles of coding in everyday activities.

THE LESSON

Using any task you can break down into step-by-step instructions, tell students to convert the instructions into computer code format, troubleshoot their "program," and ask classmates to follow the instructions step-by-step.

Here are some possible ideas:

- Clean up the classroom
- Tie a tie
- Walk around the school
- Assemble crafts
- Navigate an obstacle course on the playground or one built in class
- Perform a cultural dance or ritual
- Practice study skills
- Prepare snacks they can make in class

As students get comfortable with these exercises, challenge them to include programming principles such as loops and variables, build a class "library" for frequently used instructions, and develop a common syntax for everyone's programs.

Art by Code

THE GOAL

Teach students about graphic elements and computer-based design as they develop instructions to create a piece of art.

THE LESSON

Set up a numbered grid on a whiteboard or easel for the class, or ask the students to take out art supplies and draw their own numbered grids on graph paper. Challenge students to collectively draw a block-based object by taking turns calling out instructions. For instance, show them a picture of a simple robot and have them call out instructions to draw the robot on their own papers. The first student would say: "Select Red Crayon." The second would say: "Place Red Crayon in Box A-2." The third would say: "Go up four spaces." The fourth would say: "Go right four spaces." And so on.

MORE ADVANCED PROJECTS

- Variations on art-by-code using wood or plastic blocks, pre-cut construction paper shapes, origami, etc.
- A project involving the selection and setting aside of tools such as pencils, erasers, paintbrushes, and scissors can be a great introduction to programs such as Microsoft Paint or Photoshop.
- Introduce an important computer design concept using color-by-number worksheets. Instead of assigning the colors using their regular names, use hexadecimal color codes, like #FF0000 for red, #0000FF for blue, and #FFFF00 for yellow.

RESOURCES

- Whiteboard
- Art supplies

Binary in Beads

THE GOAL

Teach the principles of binary using arts and crafts.

THE LESSON

Teach students the basics of how binary code works.

Post a binary translation chart (see next page) and have them practice spelling words and messages in binary. Start with their names!

The Alphabet In Binary: A Translation Chart

BONUS: Let students look up additional binary codes for numbers and symbols, like "#1!" and add them to their creations.

A	01000001	J	01001010	S	01010011
a	01100001	j	01101010	s	01110011
B	01000010	K	01001011	T	01010100
b	01100010	k	01101011	t	01110100
C	01000011	L	01001100	U	01010101
c	01100011	l	01101100	u	01110101
D	01000100	M	01001101	V	01010110
d	01100100	m	01101101	v	01110110
E	01000101	N	01001110	W	01010111
e	01100101	n	01101110	w	01110111
F	01000110	O	01001111	X	01011000
f	01100110	o	01101111	x	01111000
G	01000111	P	01010000	Y	01011001
g	01100111	p	01110000	y	01111001
H	01001000	Q	01010001	Z	01011010
h	01101000	q	01110001	z	01111010
I	01001001	R	01010010		
i	01101001	r	01110010		

Using different colored beads to represent ones and zeros (*e.g.*, blue = 1, green = 0), have them string bracelets or necklaces with their names or another word or message in binary code.

Other arts and crafts forms—painting T-shirts, gluing two different kinds of macaroni, chalk on the ground, wood burning, etc.—can also be used.

RESOURCES

- Binary translation chart
- Beads of at least two different colors
- String for beading
- Other art supplies

Block-Based Code

As the coding movement grows, so does the number of popular websites designed to teach basic coding skills. While it is wonderful to have access to a variety of resources, trying to decide which ones to use can be challenging. The following sites all focus on the *block-based* approach to coding. Instead of starting beginners with text-based computer languages full of unfamiliar and intimidating symbols, these sites use visual tools and games to introduce basic concepts.

Through drag-and-drop coding and logical problem-solving, kids' confidence grows and soon they advance to more abstract and creative projects. In this section, we'll share information for some of the most popular sites. Lesson ideas will be included under the particular site in which they're most suitable for use.

Code.org (code.org)

One of the largest platforms designed to get young people coding, *Code.org* regularly releases new features and fun programs. Many feature popular kids' themes, such as *Star Wars* and *Frozen*. Students use block code to steer BB-8 or Elsa around obstacles while collecting items and dodging enemies. Age-targeted lessons help kids build skills through game-like tutorials, celebrity video lectures, classroom activities, and more.

Code.org is famous for launching the Hour of Code movement, encouraging people around the world to get basic coding exposure by learning and playing through a simple program. Beyond its online lessons and creation space, Code.org provides educational tools for teachers, connections with local schools and camps for hands-on training, and partnerships designed to spread coding knowledge everywhere computers can go.

As its offerings grow more popular, many of your incoming students will have played through its opening lessons. Guide these kids through some of Code.org's more advanced lessons, or ask them to help other students get up to speed.

Besides Hour of Code, Code.org offers partner tutorials teaching introductory coding concepts, JavaScript, and other programming languages. You can even get a curated list of teachers' one-hour coding lessons at *code.org/educate/curriculum/ teacher-led*. Here are some additional learning sites Code.org recommends:

Monster Coding (*monstercoding.com*)

Monster Coding teaches programming concepts through block-based game building and coding vocabulary lessons. Kids learn about terms, including pixels, variables, scale, random, functions, iteration, and more. Video and audio options are available with every lesson, and math and geometry lessons help reinforce what you're teaching in class.

Lightbot (*lightbot.com*)

Solve puzzles using programming logic, including instructions, procedures, and loops.

Code Monkey (*playcodemonkey.com*)

Watch out—this site can be addictive! Every stage of this game introduces a new coding concept as your monkey journeys through the jungle collecting lost bananas.

Scratch (*scratch.mit.edu*)

The block-based visual code at Scratch gives users unlimited opportunities to create games, stories, animations, calculators, and anything else they can conceive! Users can also download and work with public projects designed by other Scratch users.

For kids ages five to seven, check out the ScratchJr app for iOS and Android.

Hello Processing (*hello.processing.org*)

Learn about the intersection of code and art from high-energy video tutorials, and then use the processing program to create visual magic.

Block-Based Code Lessons and Additional Resources

Operation: Bug Swat

Submitted by James Abela (@eslweb)

THE GOAL

Students learn how to analyze and debug simple code.

THE LESSON

In small groups or on their own, students explore the Scratch Studio "Operation: Bug Swat" page (see link below).

The page features five mini-programs built using block code. Students attempt to find what is going wrong in each situation by playing the program, examining the source code, and clicking on *See Inside* to view the code. Find hints by clicking the "Answer" comment inside the code.

Once students have fixed the bugs, encourage them to reverse engineer the code and create a simple platform game of their own.

Review the program prior to sending your students there. If it's too advanced for them, try creating a simpler program of your own, building in bugs for your class to find.

RESOURCES

- *scratch.mit.edu/studios/523182*

Compare Numbers to Make a Race!

Submitted by Andrea Wilson Vazquez (@wilsandrea)

THE GOAL

Students learn to compare numbers using coding and ScratchJr.

THE LESSON

Inform your students you'll be reviewing the math concept of comparing numbers (which numbers are greater than, less than, or equal) by creating a race between different characters (sprites). Students will set up a scene with a background image and at least two sprites lined up on one side of the screen. Using block code, they'll assign a certain number of steps for each sprite to take. The sprite who travels the farthest wins. By changing the numbers, students gain a practical understanding of the concepts of greater than, less than, and equal.

RESOURCES

- iPads
- ScratchJr
- Compete Lesson Plan and Reflection Sheet available at compare.codeineveryclass.org

Coding 2D Shapes

Submitted by Steve Katz (@stevekatz)

THE GOAL

Students create and compare quadrilaterals to learn two-dimensional figures can be classified in a hierarchy based on their properties.

THE LESSON

Using the Scratch app, code a program to draw a square.

Start changing the properties of the code blocks to create different polygons.

RESOURCES

- Scratch (scratch.mit.edu)
- Instructions available at
  stevenkatz.com/blog/2016/04/13/coding-2-d-shapes

App Inventor

THE GOAL

Empower kids to develop their own mobile apps using block-based coding for the Android mobile operating system.

THE LESSON

Building apps is exciting for them and connects learning computing to familiar, real-world experiences. One great lesson on developing apps is the Hello Purr tutorial. Student can use this tutorial to build a program by clicking on an image of a cat to make it meow or purr. Challenge your students to go beyond the tutorial and figure out how to make the cat hiss in response to shaking the phone. Encourage them to discover other things they can make their cat do.

Note: Android App Inventor has some unusual bugs, often dealt with by resetting the program. On your phone, close and reopen the app. On your computer, click connect > reset connection, then connect > ai companion. Then reconnect your phone by rescanning the QR code or entering the code from the computer to the phone.

RESOURCES

MIT's Android App Inventor: *ai2.appinventor.mit.edu*
- Hello Purr Tutorial:
  appinventor.mit.edu/explore/ai2/hellopurr.html

Hopscotch (gethopscotch.com)

Hopscotch is an iOS site (usable on Macs, iPads, iPhones, and other Apple devices) and lets users design games, art programs, animations, and more. They can share their masterpieces, view and get inspired by other Hopscotchers' work, and vote for the creations they like best.

Coding Music Instrument Apps in Hopscotch

Submitted by music teacher Cheryl Burgemeister (@MRSBmusicroom)

THE GOAL

Students design musical instruments to play melody and rhythm together at the correct pitch and in time to the beat.

THE LESSON

After talking about virtual instruments, such as those found on iPad apps—GarageBand, Percussions, Real Xylophone, and Monster Chorus—ask students to create instruments using the Hopscotch app. Follow the steps at *mrsbmusicroom.com/2016/04/26/coding-music-instrument-apps-in-hopscotch*.

Students start by coding exactly the same instrument with the intention of playing together in unison from a score at the end of the lesson. Demonstrate each step, having your students coding along with you at the same time. At the end of each step, check to ensure your students have done the correct coding.

Play *Twinkle, Twinkle Little Star* together as a class, each student playing on a correctly coded melodic instrument matching the Boomwhacker notes and colors.

Encourage students to create their own instruments and music.

RESOURCES

- Hopscotch app for iPad or iPhone
- Blog post for classroom examples: *wp.me/p3OxEF-9v*
- For more teaching resources to complement this lesson, go to *bushfirepress.com/musicroom/tech/index.html*

Pencil Code (pencilcode.net)

Pencil Code is a block-based code learning site with three "playgrounds" offering super easy, fun ways to get started writing programs: draft art, create amazing music, and build stories and animations. The simplicity makes it a great tool to introduce the power of coding to your students or yourself.

Ready for more advanced play? The site has a freeplay space for creating without limits. Pencil Code is block-based, but users have the option to turn off the blocks and work directly with CoffeeScripts, a real-world programming language. CoffeeScripts is very similar to the popular JavaScript language, but it is more approachable and doesn't have the same syntax challenges.

One of the things we love about Pencil Code is it doesn't give tutorials. The program teaches by providing sample code and encouraging users to reverse engineer the code by changing and manipulating it to see what happens. Not only is this a great way to learn, it's actually how many computer programmers work. They take existing code and manipulate it to meet their own needs.

The three main learning areas ("playgrounds") offer a wealth of possibilities. From the *pencilcode.net* home page, your students will have the option to click into one of the playgrounds—Draw, Jam, and Imagine—or select the "Get Creative" website for creating their own projects.

Draw allows students to create artwork using computer programming while *Jam* is used to easily create computer programs for making music. Finally, *Imagine* lets students create stories and games with some basic computer programming.

Circle Up

THE GOAL

Demonstrate the possibility of creating different code to generate the same outcome.

THE LESSON

Using Pencil Code, ask students to create the code for a circle.

Demonstrate how to start by moving the sprite forward one, then right one, and then forward one, then right one, and then forward one and then right one, and so on. If the sprite completes this action 360 times, you'll have a circle.

Afterward ask students to work in pairs or small groups to find more efficient codes to produce the same circle. Check out the full lesson at *codeineveryclass.com/circles*.

Explore Draw

THE GOAL

Create art using computer programming.

THE LESSON

Step 1: Click the link to go to the *Draw* page.

Students will see a panel on the left filled with options for different types of art. On the right will be a box where they can drag and drop coding commands for a "sprite," in this case a turtle, that starts in the middle of the accompanying grid. This turtle sprite will execute any code instructions students create.

Step 2: Open *Line Techniques.*

Have your students select the "Line Techniques" option from the left panel, and appropriate blocks of code will appear next to the grid, including two lines of sample code.

The first command is "pen," which means the turtle is going to draw the commands given as though it were the tip of a pen. The selected color is "red," so the line will be red.

On the next line, they'll see commands reading "fd" and "100." This code means "forward one hundred pixels." When students hit the play button, the command will run: the turtle will move forward one hundred pixels, drawing a red line behind it.

Step 3: Create art!

Now it's time for your students to add more commands. To do this, they'll drag commands from the left-hand panel into the main panel. Have them start with some turns.

- Select "rt 90" (right turn, 90 degrees) and drag it to line 3.
- Drag "fd 100" to line 4.
- Drag "rt 90" to line 5.
- Drag "fd 100" to line 6.

- Drag "rt 90" to line 7.
- Drag "fd 100" to line 8.

Students hit the play button to run the program. The turtle will go forward, turn right, go forward, turn right, and so on, until it's drawn a square!

Students just wrote code, made a computer sprite execute commands, and created artwork—all while practicing some basic math and geometry concepts.

Step 4: Learn more about it.

At the bottom of the screen are several tags students can click to learn more about the various commands and programming concepts they used in the task. Have them check these out and use what they've learned to build more and better code.

Explore Jam

THE GOAL

Students learn music principles while coding a familiar melody.

THE LESSON

Step 1: Click the link to go to the *Jam* page.

On this page, students will see a panel on the left with links to various music tools. On the right will be a code entry box, with the same turtle and grid beside it. Tell students to experiment with Jam using a sample song to see how the code works.

Step 2: Select the option *A Simple Tune.*

This sample code will be in text form instead of block-based. Your students will see code that says:

p = new piano

The next line says

p, play G G D' D' E' E'

This means the new piano is playing those notes; and, sure enough, when students hit *Play* to run the command, they can see the piano keys play the notes.

A message at the top of the screen encourages users to experiment with the notes and complete the *Twinkle, Twinkle Little Star* tune. Your students can experiment:

- Change the second D' to just D. When they play it, they'll hear the tone has changed. In fact, the D with the apostrophe is an octave higher than the regular D, which implies the apostrophe controls the tone. Ask your students what they think will happen if they add two apostrophes to a D.
- Add a second apostrophe and hit play. Now they can hear the really high D! Sure enough, two apostrophes made the D sound two octaves higher.

This is a great way for students to learn how to code. They look at the code, run it, and then experiment, tweaking the code and seeing what changes as a result.

Explore Imagine

THE GOAL

Students create stories using branching logic and variables.

THE LESSON

Step 1: Click the link to go to the *Imagine* page.

Students will see options in a left-hand panel, and a code box and a turtle grid for their programs on the right.

Step 2: Experience an interactive story.

Similar to the Choose Your Own Adventure™ books, your students can learn to create their own stories using branching logic. Students select the "Tree Climbing" option then click the Play button. The program will tell them: "You are in a field with a tree." Below it, a clickable button will say: "Climb up." When they click it, the next stage of the program will give students two choices: climb up or climb down. They can choose the one they want then keep progressing through the story, experimenting with clicking different buttons in different orders.

Step 3: Learn branching logic.

Tell your students to play through again, but this time, try to connect what's happening with the code on the left with what's happening as they move through the program on the right. This will be a simple introduction to branching logic.

Step 4: Create their own!

Encourage students to play with options, adding or removing branches, changing the text of the story, dropping in images, and otherwise creating their own interactive stories. When they're finished, use a screencasting tool to record and share their work!

::

Block-Based Coding in 3-D

Submitted by Amanda Voth

THE GOAL

Students learn the basics of drag-and-drop coding and logical problem-solving using both digital and real-world tools.

THE LESSON

Students use blocks, tiles, and mini-figures to recreate the grid and sprites used by block-based coding websites. Using these tools, they create 3D versions of a computer program, helping them visualize what code directions they'll need to use.

Take this lesson up a notch by using life-size floor tiles and encouraging students to "put themselves in the puzzle."

RESOURCES

- Computer with Internet access
- Any block-based code site
- Blocks or tiles (math manipulatives, square floor tiles)
- Mini-figures (LEGO, action figures, toys)

Block-Based Coding Club

THE GOAL

Promote collaboration and foster a persistence-focused learning environment.

THE LESSON

Set up a club where students can use their free time in class, study periods, or after-school hours to play with coding projects.

Provide structure and lessons through a block-based code website, with students demonstrating mastery of its curriculum before proposing projects of their own.

Motivate and support them by:

- offering real-world and virtual rewards for completing activities and projects
- offering classroom credit for projects related to their academics
- leading tutorials on special programming tools
- bringing in professional coders from the community
- taking on meaningful projects to help the community
- working on projects with peers throughout the community and around the world
- taking part in coding competitions
- leading field trips to see coding at work in the world

Hackathon-Lite

Submitted by Scott Moss (@scotthmoss)

THE GOAL

Students apply their current coding skills to simple challenges then compare their different strategies.

THE LESSON

Hackathon Lite is much like a math warm-up activity, but can last much longer. Students are given a description for a program to create within a given time. Tasks can range from "make the sprite draw a square" to "create a game where the user must guess a number between one and one hundred."

Ask your students to come up with multiple ways to perform a single task. After completion, review all of the various techniques students used to create their programs. Try not to judge work as "better" or "worse," but discuss factors such as flexibility and reusability of code.

You can include bonus tasks for students ready to push themselves to the next level. In the prior example, for instance, students could code the program to respond to user input, telling the user to guess higher or lower.

Branching Logic

The "Tree Climbing" adventure from Pencil Code uses branching logic, one of the most useful concepts to understand when you are new to computer programming. When you design a computer program to have users make choices that change the outcomes the program provides, you're using branching logic.

Besides working well for telling stories, branching logic is a great tool for organizing logical structures, developing websites and forms, building study guides, and narrowing down options from a large field of possibilities.

Here are some lessons to help you teach branching logic.

Branching Logic Story Map

THE GOAL

Introduce the concept of branching logic while engaging students in the processes of story creation and website building.

THE LESSON

Start by mapping out a story narrative using a whiteboard or a wall with sticky notes. Create a character, setting, and situation, and give the character two choices. Your students contribute ideas for what happens next based on each choice. Make sure they come up with at least two choices for each path. The more options they offer, the more complicated the story gets. The map gets bigger and bigger—like a tree with many branches—thus the name "branching" logic. Show students how the options branch off of each other, occasionally reconnect, and/or lead from different "limbs" to the same "leaves," or conclusions.

Students can use coding to build an online adventure book. Assign students to manage each branch of the adventure story.

They can create a separate Google Forms page to use branching logic. First, create individual sections within the form for each branch of the story. Then, set the multiple choice options within each section to direct readers to the appropriate branch of the story based on the options they select. Alternatively, they can use Google Sites to create a web page for each branch. Each page should feature the story text, an image, and at least two choices. Each choice should link to a new page, allowing the reader to make a decision about where the story goes next. (Of course, as noted above, some of the branches will link back to earlier points on the "limb"—or may even lead to dead ends!)

Don't forget to test the links!

RESOURCES
- Whiteboard
- Google Forms—Students use multiple choice questions to enable the "Go to page based on answer" feature. Check out detailed instructions here: *goo.gl/7pzqyH*
- Google Sites—Create a site for your story and a naming system for the pages (for example: *www.anytownschools. org/TeacherName/StoryTitle/Intro.html, /Branch1.html, / Branch2.html,* and so on). The Introduction page launches the story and includes two links at the bottom, each one leading to a different page.

Branching Logic Plant Identification

THE GOAL
Explore branching logic and build environmental awareness by creating an app to help users identify local plant life through a series of questions.

THE LESSON

This lesson works with any branching logic system. Your students can work with notebooks, Google Forms, Google Sites, Pencil Code, App Inventor, etc. Start by asking your students to identify all the plants in a specific area of your campus or neighborhood. If there's high density and diversity of plant life in the area, either narrow the space they're examining, have students select only certain types of plants, or limit the number of potential plant options in some other way.

Using Wikipedia, students divide the plants by different visual criteria, such as a tree versus a bush. Each criterium then has subcategories. For example, is it a deciduous tree losing its leaves in the autumn or a conifer with needles and cones? If deciduous, what shape are its leaves? And students can add additional branching criteria.

Students enter the various categories and subcategories into the notebooks or other branching-logic system and include links to relevant web pages. They then test their work using the questions to see if they can accurately identify each plant species.

Resources

- Google Sites (*sites.google.com*)
- Google Forms (*forms.google.com*)
- Pencil Code (*pencilcode.net*)
- MIT App Inventor (*appinventor.mit.edu*)

Code in Unusual Places

Genetic Code versus Binary Code

THE GOAL

Deepen understanding of the similarities and differences between genetic and binary code.

THE LESSON

Teach students the basics of how binary code works (see page 83 for a simple overview). Compare binary code instructions to genetic code:

- Binary has two *bits*: 1 and 0. DNA has four *bits*: the base nucleotides of adenine (A), guanine (G), cytosine (C), and thymine (T). Hand out (or instruct students to build) different sets of colored blocks to represent the bits for each code.

- Genetic sequences involve *codons*, combinations of three nucleotides, to deliver chunks of information. Binary languages also use chunking. How many three-part combinations of ones and zeroes can your students find? How many three-part combinations of AGCT nucleotides can they find? Can they be sure they've found all the combinations? This is a great opportunity to use charts (like this one at *hyperphysics. phy-astr.gsu.edu/hbase/organic/gencode.html*) and explore math concepts such as exponents.

- The genetic code uses several different codons to communicate "stop" and one codon serving as both a "start" and an amino acid. What structures do binary languages use to tell machines how to read them?

- What are some advantages and disadvantages to having just two bits of information to work with instead of four, or strings of three bits as opposed to, say, eight? What might happen if people decided to start writing machine code using a four-bit system like DNA? How would this be different from creating a life form? More advanced students can explore the current research on these models together, including the exciting advances in quantum computing.

- Review the parallels between genetic code and binary code. Do these similarities mean humans are just giant computers? Or are electronic devices miniature living things?

RESOURCES
- Colored blocks or supplies for making them
- Supplies for making charts

Tip Calculator

THE GOAL
Students use data and spreadsheets to learn essential coding knowledge.

THE LESSON
Armed with this simple algebra formula, students calculate a tip for a restaurant bill:

$$t=b*r$$
$$t=tip$$
$$b=bill$$
$$r=tip\ rate\ (15\%,\ 18\%,\ or\ 20\%)$$

Students create a tip calculator app in a spreadsheet by following the instructions here: *goo.gl/dEHHkI*. Have students share the spreadsheet online so anyone with the link can edit.

By building the formula into a programming lesson, the variables become interactive. Seeing the numbers change in real time not only helps students grasp the math concepts, but they'll also have the satisfaction of having actually built a useful tool using algebra.

RESOURCES

- Microsoft Excel or Google Sheets (Excel works fine for this project, but Sheets are much easier to share.)

8-Bit Coding

Submitted by Arielle Goldstein (@ArielleTeach)

THE GOAL

Students work with 8-bit art and game design and coding with arrows.

THE LESSON

Students play Space Invaders and try to determine its basic codes.

Step 1: Design an 8-bit Space Invaders character on a piece of graph paper.

Step 2: Create a code to recreate their character online.

Step 3: Add codes to change the character's size and color.

Step 4: Test out other students' codes!

Step 5: [Teachers] Create a game in Scratch using the students' character designs.

Step 6: [Teachers] Build real-life versions of characters using a 3D printer to use in future coding lessons.

RESOURCES

- *pacxon4u.com/space-invaders*
- Graph paper
- Scratch (optional)
- 3D printer (optional)

Coding Gets Physical

Build Your Own Computer

THE GOAL

Students experience hands-on programming of a simple computer using Arduino or Raspberry Pi.

THE LESSON

Using an Arduino starter kit (available at *goo.gl/ZGdXAZ*) to understand the basics, absolute beginners can learn to program their own computers. Arduino uses simple repetitive tasks such as opening and closing a garage door, reading the outside temperature and reporting it to Twitter, or driving a simple robot. For more advanced programmers who need a full-fledged computer to control a more complicated robot, perform multiple tasks using multiple inputs, or conduct intense calculations over time, Raspberry Pi is a better option.

Regardless of which option you choose for your class, check out *raspberrypi.org*. Students can follow online lessons and video tutorials to guide them in creating their own programs. Encourage students to explore further on the hundreds of forums for Arduino and Raspberry Pi enthusiasts.

RESOURCES

- Arduino
- Raspberry Pi

From Bach to Bytes

Submitted by Joe Park

THE GOAL

Students learn how principles of music and coding overlap by exploring samples, loops, and instructions in SonicPi, using either a Raspberry Pi or traditional computer.

THE LESSON

Introduce SonicPi to students using a live coding demonstration. (For a great introduction to SonicPi, we highly recommend the Raspberry Pi Foundations step-by-step instructions at raspberrypi.org/learning/sonic-pi-lessons.)

Show them a screencast tutorial for using the play, samples, and live loop functions.

Assign students to create a musical composition of their own using all three of these functions. The composition must be original and one to two minutes in length.

Have students share their work!

RESOURCES

- Raspberry Pi or traditional computer
- SonicPi software

Robotics with MINDSTORMS

THE GOAL

Students build a robot army.

THE LESSON

Even the greatest robot army needs to start somewhere, and LEGO has come up with a terrific launch point. Their MINDSTORMS line of electronic robots is a great platform for teaching students to design, build, and code their own robots to respond to the environment. (Please tell them to use their power for good.)

The line features robot construction kits allowing users to build dozens of different robot configurations. Students can learn to program their robots using apps, games, and challenges, all with the help of community forums and customer support.

Caution: MINDSTORMS sets are not cheap. A single kit runs about $350. You might want to start this lesson project by running a bake sale...

RESOURCES
- LEGO MINDSTORMS (*goo.gl/DJWq46*)

Going the Distance

Submitted by Andrew McDonald (@afmcdnl)

THE GOAL

Using MINDSTORMS robots, students investigate concepts of speed, distance, and time.

THE LESSON

Place a toy figure at a set distance from a starting line. Students drive their robot up to the figure but don't actually touch it. The closer a robot gets to the figure without touching it, the higher the score.

Step 1: Students design a robot to drive forward and program it to be able to stop after one second, two seconds, three seconds, and so on.

Step 2: Students measure how far the robot travels in one second and predict how far they think the robot will go after longer periods of time.

Step 3: Students test the program. How far does the robot travel each time? Have students record these values in a table.

Step 4: Challenge students to find any patterns in the data. Is there a formula to predict the time required to go any given distance? Have them predict the amount of time their robots will need in order to travel the exact distance from the starting line to where the toy figure is placed.

Step 5: Students program their robots with their predictions.

Step 6: Experiment with the predictions. Were they correct? What did they learn about momentum and graphing slope? What could have improved their final result?

Don't forget to take photos or videos along the way!

RESOURCES
- MINDSTORMS programmable robots
- Tape measure

Sphero Hero Challenge
Submitted by Laurie Guyon (@guyonsmile)

THE GOAL
Students use Sphero robots to understand the Hero's Journey and how it relates to the protagonist of a story they are currently reading.

The Lesson
Start by teaching students about the Hero's Journey. Here are two great videos on this concept, along with links to full lessons:
- *youtu.be/KGV1BvnyvGo*
- *youtu.be/Hhk4N9A0oCA*

Have students create a real-world model of the journey: an obstacle course representing different experiences along the way, for example.

Ask them to code a Sphero robot to navigate the course. Sphero robots are app-enabled, ball-shaped creations, and can be programmed to perform any number of tasks. (Yes, some are designed to look like BB-8 from *Star Wars!*)

Discuss the challenges the main character overcame at this part of his or her journey.

Bonus: Have students film different parts of the lesson and create a culminating video to share.

RESOURCES

- Sphero robot (*sphero.com/sphero*)
- Any materials available to create the challenges (buckets, ramps, cups, plastic blocks, etc.)
- iPad for recording

Writing with a Pro-Bot
Submitted by Margaret Volak

THE GOAL

Students code a race-car-shaped robot to create letters with its movements.

THE LESSON

A Pro-Bot is a simple, car-shaped robot with a back-mounted code entry pad. It's a 3-D version of the traditional Logo programming tool (a turtle sprite that can be moved around a screen based on simple code). The Pro-Bot can move in different directions, for different distances, and turn particular angles when necessary. Its felt-tipped pen holder can be programmed to lift or go down and trace a line marking its path.

For this lesson, assign students in small groups (Coding Crews) to draw a single letter using the Pro-Bot.

Step 1: Using graph paper, students plan the steps involved in drawing the letter.

Step 2: Students design a code letting the Pro-Bot draw it. They may need to test their code using a toy car before running the program.

Step 3: With marker tool deployed, students set the Pro-Bot into motion and see their letter come to life!

Step 4: Each Coding Crew team adds their letter to a display and posts the code for creating it on an index card underneath.

Step 5: Students put their individual letters together, rearranging them to figure out the "Mystery Word" or phrase—a vocabulary word, a school character trait, an upcoming holiday, etc.

Check out the full lesson plan here: *codeineveryclass.com/probot.*

RESOURCES
- Graph paper
- Tape measure (optional)
- Pro-Bot
- Construction paper
- Marker
- Record sheet and index card

Exploring Computing Concepts

These lessons let students peek behind the curtain and learn real-life computer programming skills.

Input-Output and Math Fact Checking with Python

Submitted by Andrea Wilson Vazquez (@wilsandrea)

THE GOAL

Students use the Python programming language and their knowledge of math facts, input-output rules, and cause/effect relationships to create a math-fact-checking tool.

THE LESSON

Access the lesson plan at *inout.codeineveryclass.org*. **Note**: This lesson works best for those who have some experience working with Python.

Step 1: Review input/output tables with math facts. Discuss connections to cause/effect.

Step 2: Introduce Python syntax.

Step 3: Familiarize students with Python's conditional syntax and commands through a Python Conditional Go Fish Activity (included in lesson plan).

Step 4: Use Python syntax and commands learned in Go Fish activity to create a math fact-checking game. Use the website *trinket.io* to do coding.

Step 5: Students do a gallery walk to beta test each other's fact-checking games.

RESOURCES

- Lesson Plan available at *inout.codeineveryclass.org*
- Python Conditionals Go Fish Activity (link included in lesson)

Expose the Code!

THE GOAL

Connect students with the code underlying their favorite websites, and deepen their understanding of the power of code.

THE LESSON

Students pick a favorite website, right-click on the page, and select "View page source."

Analyze the code. What do they notice? Based on what they've learned about code so far, can they identify the programming language? The elements of syntax? Can they find the original content within the syntax structure? What gets repeated?

Visit a very simple web page, like this one at *https:// en.wikipedia.org/wiki/Sock*, or perhaps one you've built with HTML. Instruct students to view this page source and describe what they see.

Using a simple web page builder, how much of each page can they recreate on their own?

THE RESOURCES

- Google Sites or another web page builder

Using Variables in Coding

THE GOAL

Students learn about variables and logical structure by programming a game to help children learn about objects, colors, and languages.

THE LESSON

Students develop a children's game where users can learn the names of several different objects and colors in several different languages. The objects, colors, and languages are the variables.

They'll need the following elements:

- a chart organizing the variables by category (objects, colors, languages)
- a way to rotate through each set of variables
- a field to display the names for the object and color
- a logical, step-by-step program controlling the game using block-based coding

For instance, a user opens the program and presses a button labeled "Change Shape." An object appears and cycles through the shapes of a triangle, a circle, and a square. Once they've chosen an object to display, they move to the next button: "Change Color." Now they change the object's color to blue, yellow, or red.

The user then presses a button marked "Choose Language" and selects one of three languages: English, French, or Spanish.

When the user presses the final button, the program checks what the current values for each of the variables. If it's a blue square and the language is Spanish, a caption will appear reading: "*Un cuadrado azul.*" If it's a yellow circle and the language is French, the caption will read: "*Un cercle jaune.*"

Encourage students to share their work with the class and see how creative they were with their object, color, and language choices and their code!

RESOURCES

Any block-based programming tool: Code.org, Scratch, Hopscotch, etc.

Minecraft as Mentor

THE GOAL

Explore computing or academic topics through a teacher-designed version of Minecraft.

THE LESSON

Minecraft is an online creative sandbox that offers infinite opportunities for open-ended design play. Users can build anything from castles to actual working computers.

Check out Minecraft Education Edition at *MinecraftEdu.com*. Designed by teachers but officially supported by the Minecraft (and now Microsoft) team, it's more appropriate for classroom use and provides a number of helpful bonuses:

- Classroom management tools
- Multiplayer environment
- Student moderation tools
- Library of teacher-created lessons and activities
- Custom blocks for classroom usage
- Safety design for use with school proxy servers, firewalls, etc.

Besides coding, Minecraft Education Edition can be used as a platform for teaching lessons on almost any topic.

Science and Math: Measure velocity by running carts down slopes at different angles.

Technology: Build a holiday lights display using Redstone and command blocks.

Art and English: Recreate scenes from books and films by building them and recording characters reliving the events.

History and Geography: Explore and build scale models of famous world sites and structures.

RESOURCES
- Minecraft Education Edition
- Join the community at *education.minecraft.net*

A Call to Action

By reading this book and incorporating some of its ideas and lessons into your curriculum, you're joining a movement of tens of thousands of teachers who are committed to a brighter, healthier, and more sustainable future. You've learned so much about the power coding has to shape both technology fluency and logical thinking skills. You've seen the demand for skilled programmers at every level and across major career fields, and this insight makes you appreciate how great an impact coding can have on students' job prospects. You know how computer literacy and acquiring coding skills can level the playing field for children of different racial, ethnic, and socioeconomic backgrounds and the importance of encouraging students' passion for technology regardless of gender or race.

Don't let your enthusiasm for coding in the classroom get lost in the shuffle of daily demands. Set aside and protect a regular block of time for planning curriculum, exploring new tech devices and learning, learning websites, and practicing skills you'd like to share. Feel free to enlist your students in the effort! Get involved and stay involved with other twenty-first century education leaders. We need communities to inspire us to keep growing, learning, and collaborating. Belonging to a network of education and technology enthusiasts keeps us current with the excellent new tools and learning ideas!

If you can convey only one takeaway to those worried about implementing coding in the classroom, assure them most code-related lessons can be implemented in *any* subject without fundamentally changing the class goals. In fact, shifting teaching practices to involve technology and programming often leads to stronger academic learning outcomes. Actually, we believe coding skills are some of the most important gifts we can give our students in twenty-first century education to help them—and our planet—to thrive.

The world has seen tremendous change in the past few decades, with new technology transforming the landscape every few years and leading to radical shifts in our social institutions and daily lives. While much of this change has been positive, many of the devices and processes introduced during the past one hundred years have had unintended consequences—from political upheaval to environmental destruction on a global scale.

Today we have two choices: slam on the brakes or clean up our mess. Our vote is to use the best social and technological advancements to support our students *and* our planet for years to come. It's a daunting task, and educators are on the front lines. If you feel overwhelmed by the challenges before us, focus on the tremendous opportunities new tech brings. Technology isn't just another challenging tool to learn. It's an incredible resource, helping us in our daily work, connecting us with fellow educators, and providing our students with opportunities for meaningful learning and collaboration that were previously unavailable. These are the skills and tools our students need to make the world a better place, and we have an obligation to ensure what we're teaching them has relevance in the world they're facing.

As we've noted, our goal for beginner coders is to build their familiarity with technology and their confidence with coding. Along the way, they'll develop skills in logic and analysis. For those with advanced experience, our goal is to integrate technology with both educational curriculum and real-world problem-solving. We want these students to get fired up about the amazing developments in tech and all the ways they can make a significant impact *right now* on some of the major challenges facing the planet. We want them so connected with resources and leaders, they're able to journey from meaningful educational experiences right into great work. Most of all, we want them to be inspired to share the power of coding in ways that make a difference for their communities and the world.

While this sounds like a tall order, these achievements grow over time from seeds planted in the simplest of exercises. In this way, coding is just like alphabet games and book reports leading to careers in marketing and politics or counting games and geometric models leading students to become accountants and architects.

So dive in! Lead your students to take their first steps of discovery. Then give them a decade or two. We can't wait to see what grows from your seeds!

It's Time for Code in Every Class

You have the teaching tools.

You're connected with the worldwide EdTech community.

You have the knowledge to share coding with your students—*all* your students.

Now it's time to go forward and inspire the next generation! Give them the tools to dive in to tech-powered adventures. Set them on the path to wow us all. Help them build a better world!

And always remember that coding is for everyone. For boys. For girls. For kids of every color, creed, and culture. For kids with their own personal fleet of devices, and kids who've never had tech of their own.

And coding is for you.

Go learn! Go teach! Go create!

Then come back and share.

We'll see you in the future!

Resources

Communities for Technology Educators

Code in Every Class **community on Twitter** — *#codeineveryclass*,
@brookhouser
> Join the conversation and share what you're learning and
> teaching.

EdTechTeam Global Google+ Community —
community.codeineveryclass.com

20time community — *20time.org*
> To learn more about twenty-first century capstone projects
> and to access many resources, visit the website and check out
> book, *The 20time Project*.

Google Apps for Education — *google.com/edu/apps*
> GAFE targets the education market with deep support for
> launching and maintaining school-based Chromebook fleets
> while boosting creative and collaborative learning. The system
> provides productivity tools, classroom management systems,
> programming for educators and students, and affordable access
> to devices (Chromebooks and tablets). It also manages secu-
> rity and updates, and makes setup for entire device fleets sim-
> ple, while offering tens of thousands of educator-vetted apps,
> books, and videos—all in a communication-friendly space.

GAFEsummit — *gafesummit.com*
> Attend a high intensity two-day EdTechTeam Global Summit
> near you. These are incredible professional development events

to supercharge your classroom and connect you with other amazing educators.

Coder Dojo — *coderdojo.com*

Global network of free, independent, volunteer-led computer programming clubs for young people.

Books for Deeper Learning

Code: The Hidden Language of Computer Hardware and Software by Charles Petzold

Computational Thinking, Coding and Robotics in the Classroom: A Guide for Teachers by Kevin Cummins

CodEd: Teaching Coding in the Classroom Kindle Edition by Kristopher Linus Velez

Coding for Kids from the *For Dummies* series by Camille McCue

Drive: The Surprising Truth About What Motivates Us by Daniel H. Pink

Mindset: The New Psychology of Success by Carol Dweck

Most Likely To Succeed: Preparing Our Kids for the Innovation Era by Tony Wagner and Ted Dintersmith

Programming in the Primary Grades: Beyond the Hour of Code by Sam Patterson

Block-Based Code Sites for K–12+ Learners

App Inventor—*appinventor.mit.edu*

Use the simple block-based builder to develop your own programs for Android mobile devices.

Code.org—*code.org*

This computer science education and advocacy site includes block-based coding games, coder communities, and partnerships.

Code Monkey—*playcodemonkey.com*

This is a terrifically illustrated learning game. Students advance through a journey of stages as they learn both block-based and text-based coding skills and vocabulary.

Hopscotch—*gethopscotch.com* / App Store

Users can design games, art, animations, and play in the sandbox of this iOS app.

Lightbot—*lightbot.com*

Solve puzzles using programming logic, including instructions, procedures, and loops.

Monster Coding—*monstercoding.com*

Block-based games and lessons help kids learn the terms and techniques of coding.

Pencil Code—*pencilcode.net*

Pencil is a collaborative programming site for drawing art, playing music, creating games, and experimenting with math and code.

Scratch—*scratch.mit.edu*

Free programming language site for creating interactive stories, games, and animations.

Coding Through Art

Hello Processing—*hello.processing.org*

Series of video tutorials and exercises teaching programming using stunning visuals.

Chrome Music Lab—*musiclab.chromeexperiments.com/About*

Collaborative music/code experiments in Web Audio API exploring how music works.

Sonic Pi—*sonic-pi.net*

Use this resource to create professional-grade music with code.

Hardware

Cubetto—*primotoys.com*

Cubetto is a wooden robot whose movements are controlled by the placement of wooden blocks as code (hands-on coding for ages three and up).

LEGO MINDSTORMS—*mindstorms.lego.com*

Find construction and software kits for building custom, programmable robots.

Raspberry Pi—*raspberrypi.org*

A tiny, affordable computer for learning programming through fun, practical projects—Check out the Raspberry Pi website for hundreds of inspiring project ideas and guides.

Arduino—*arduino.cc*

An even tinier affordable computer for learning programming

Classes in Coding and Beyond

Khan Academy (Free)—*khanacademy.org*
Nonprofit educational site with free courses on computer science and more

Lynda.com ($)—*lynda.com*
Online educational resource with classes on software, coding, and more

Code School ($)—*codeschool.com*
Online classes in software, programming, and computing

Codecademy ($)—*codecademy.com*
Bite-sized lessons in popular programming languages, accessible to middle schoolers and older

Computer Programming for Girls

The following sites include great resources for learning about code, terrific models for young computer programmers, and potential connections with local women coders who can help teach lessons and walk students through the world of coding.

Black Girls Code—*blackgirlscode.com*

Girls Who Code—*girlswhocode.com*

Girl Develop It—*girldevelopit.com*

Women in Technology International—*witi.com*

Anita Borg Institute for Women and Technology—*anitaborg.org*

The Association for Women in Computing—*awc-hq.org/home.html*

National Center for Women & Information Technology—*ncwit.org*

LinuxChix—*linuxchix.org*

Systers email list—*systers.org*

Boosting Computer Programming for Minority Groups

Code2040—*code2040.org*

Access, awareness, and opportunities for top Black and Latino/Latina engineering talent to ensure their leadership in tech

iD Tech Camps—*idtech.com*

Educational summer camps across the U.S. teaching subjects such as computer programming, digital video production, and robotics

#yeswecode—*yeswecode.org*

Boosts opportunities for young people of color in tech fields by growing the pipeline and building connections

ConnectED Initiative—*tech.ed.gov/connected*

President Obama's initiative to bring cutting-edge educational technologies, devices, and training to 99 percent of U.S. schools by 2018

Level Playing Field Institute—*lpfi.org*

Nonprofit focused on eliminating barriers to diversity in STEM fields, including technology

Black Founders—*blackfounders.com*

Nonprofit dedicated to increasing the number of black tech entrepreneurs

What's Happening with Computer Science and Education

Code.org Statistics—*codeineveryclass.org/sourcedata*

This document maintained by Code.org shares a fascinating summary of current data related to coding, coding jobs, and coding education in America.

Most Likely to Succeed: Preparing Our Kids for the Innovation Era—*tonywagner.com/1933* and *mltsfilm.org*

The book and film by Tony Wagner and Ted Dintersmith explain how to fix our educational system by shifting from a factory focus to one of creative problem-solving.

"Don't Learn To Code. Learn To Think." by Yevgeniy Brikman—*ybrikman.com/writing/2014/05/19/dont-learn-to-code-learn-to-think*

This 2014 article is one of the best treatises on the value of computational thinking available.

Computing at School—*computingatschool.org.uk*

See what's possible with a nationwide embrace of coding. Computing at School is a regional-hub system used by the United Kingdom to bring computer science to all its schools.

MORE BOOKS FROM EDTECHTEAM PRESS
edtechteam.com/books

The HyperDoc Handbook
Digital Lesson Design Using Google Apps

By Lisa Highfill, Kelly Hilton, and Sarah Landis

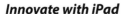

The HyperDoc Handbook is a practical reference guide for all K–12 educators who want to transform their teaching into blended-learning environments. *The HyperDoc Handbook* is a bestselling book that strikes the perfect balance between pedagogy and how-to tips while also providing ready-to-use lesson plans to get you started with HyperDocs right away.

Innovate with iPad
Lessons to Transform Learning in the Classroom

By Karen Lirenman and Kristen Wideen

Written by two primary teachers, this book provides a complete selection of clearly explained, engaging, open-ended lessons to change the way you use iPad with students at home or in the classroom. It features downloadable task cards, student-created examples, and extension ideas to use with your students. Whether you have access to one iPad for your entire class or one for each student, these lessons will help you transform learning in your classroom.

The Space
A Guide for Educators

By Rebecca Louise Hare and Robert Dillon

The Space supports the conversation around revolution happening in education today concerning the reshaping of school spaces. This book goes well beyond the ideas for learning-space design that focuses on Pinterest-perfect classrooms and instead discusses real and practical ways to design learning spaces that support and drive learning.

Classroom Management in the Digital Age
Effective Practices for Technology-Rich Learning Spaces

By Patrick Green and Heather Dowd

Classroom Management in the Digital Age helps guide and support teachers through the new landscape of device-rich classrooms. It provides practical strategies to novice and expert educators alike who want to maximize learning and minimize distraction. Learn how to keep up with the times while limiting time wasters and senseless screen-staring time.

The Google Apps Guidebook
Lessons, Activities, and Projects Created by Students for Teachers

By Kern Kelley and the Tech Sherpas

The Google Apps Guidebook is filled with great ideas for the classroom from the voice of the students themselves. Each chapter introduces an engaging project that teaches students (and teachers) how to use one of Google's powerful tools. Projects are differentiated for a variety of age ranges and can be adapted for most content areas.

Making Your School Something Special
Enhance Learning, Build Confidence, and Foster Success at Every Level

By Rushton Hurley

In *Making Your School Something Special*, educator and international speaker Rushton Hurley explores the mindsets, activities, and technology that make for great learning. You'll learn how to create strong learning activities and make your school a place where students and teachers alike want to be—because it's where they feel energized, inspired and special.

Making Your Teaching Something Special
50 Simple Ways to Become a Better Teacher

By Rushton Hurley

In the second book in his series, Rushton Hurley highlights key areas of teaching that play a part in shaping your success as an educator. Whether you are finding your way as a brand new teacher or are a seasoned teacher who is looking for some powerful ideas, this book offers inspiration and practical advice to help you make this year your best yet.

The Google Cardboard Book
Explore, Engage, and Educate with Virtual Reality

An EdTechTeam Collaboration

In *The Google Cardboard Book*, EdTechTeam trainers and leaders offer step-by-step instructions on how to use virtual reality technology in your classroom—no matter what subject you teach. You'll learn what tools you need (and how affordable they can be), which apps to start with, and how to view, capture, and share 360° videos and images.

Transforming Libraries
A Toolkit for Innovators, Makers, and Seekers

By Ron Starker

In the Digital Age, it's more important than ever for libraries to evolve into gathering points for collaboration, spaces for innovation, and places where authentic learning occurs. In *Transforming Libraries*, Ron Starker reveals ways to make libraries makerspaces, innovation centers, community commons, and learning design studios that engage multiple forms of intelligence.

Intention
Critical Creativity in the Classroom

By Amy Burvall and Dan Ryder

Inspiring and exploring creativity opens pathways for students to use creative expression to demonstrate content knowledge, critical thinking, and the problem solving that will serve them best no matter what their futures may bring. *Intention* offers a collection of ideas, activities, and reasons for bringing creativity to every lesson.

The Conference Companion
Sketchnotes, Doodles, and Creative Play for Teaching and Learning

By Becky Green

Wherever you are learning, whatever your doodle comfort level, this jovial notebook is your buddy. Sketchnotes, doodles, and creative play await both you and your students. Part workshop, part journal, and part sketchbook, these simple and light-hearted scaffolds and lessons will transform your listening and learning experiences while providing creative inspiration for your classroom.

Bring the World to Your Classroom
Using Google Geo Tools

By Kelly Kermode and Kim Randall

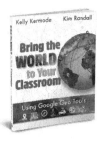

We live and work in a global society, but many students have only a very small community or neighborhood as their frame of reference. Expand their horizons and help them increase their understanding of how they fit in the global landscape using Google Geo Tools. This book is packed full of how-tos and sample projects to get you and your learners moving forward with mapping, exploring, and making connections to the world around you.

50 Ways to Use YouTube in the Classroom

By Patrick Green

Your students are already accessing YouTube, so why not meet them where they are as consumers of information? By using the tools they choose, you can maximize their understanding in ways that matter. *50 Ways to Use YouTube in the Classroom* is an accessible guide that will improve your teaching, your students' learning, and your classroom culture.

Illuminate
Technology Enhanced Learning

By Bethany Petty

In *Illuminate*, author, educator, and technology trainer Bethany Petty explains how to use technology to improve your students' learning experiences. You'll learn specific how-tos for using a wide variety of apps and tools as well as the why behind using technology. Meet your students' needs and make learning memorable using technology enhanced learning.

The Martians in Your Classroom
STEM in Every Learning Space

By Rachael Mann and Stephen Sandford

In *The Martians in Your Classroom*, educator Rachael Mann and former Director of Space Technology Exploration at NASA Stephen Sandford reveal the urgent need for science, technology, engineering, and math (STEM) and career and technical education (CTE) in every learning space. Proposing an international endeavor to stimulate students' interest in science and technology, they highlight the important roles educators, business leaders, and politicians can play in advancing STEM in schools.

More Now

A Message from the Future for the Educators of Today

By Mark Wagner, PhD

The priorities and processes of education must change if we are going to prepare students for their future. In *More Now*, EdTechTeam Founder Mark Wagner, explores the six essential elements of effective school change: courageous leaders, empowered teachers, student agency, inspiring spaces, robust infrastructure, and engaged communities. You'll learn from educational leaders, teachers, and technologists how you can make each of these essential elements part of your school or district culture—starting *now*.

40 Ways to Inject Creativity into Your Classroom with Adobe Spark

By Ben Forta and Monica Burns

Experienced educators Ben Forta and Monica Burns offer step-by-step guidance on how to incorporate this powerful tool into your classroom in ways that are meaningful and relevant. They present 40 fun and practical lesson plans suitable for a variety of ages and subjects as well as 15 graphic organizers to get you started. With the tips, suggestions, and encouragement in this book, you'll find everything you need to inject creativity into your classroom using Adobe Spark.

The Top 50 Chrome Extensions for the Classroom

By Christopher Craft, PhD

If you've ever wished there were a way to add more minutes to the day, Chrome Extensions just may be the answer. In *The Top 50 Chrome Extensions for the Classroom*, you'll learn time-saving tips and efficiency tricks that will help reduce the amount of time spent in lesson preparation and administrative tasks—so you can spend more time with students.

About the Authors

KEVIN BROOKHOUSER, M.ED.
is the author of *The 20time Project: How Educators Can Launch Google's Formula for Future-Ready Students*. He teaches project-based learning, digital citizenship, and design at York School in Monterey, California, and is a Google for Education Certified Innovator and Certified Trainer and National Association of Independent
Schools Teacher of the Future. Kevin serves on the board of The International School of Monterey. He is a learning animal. Connect at *kevinbrookhouser.com*.

RIA MEGNIN is an author, editor, and former writing instructor. She has edited and co-written four books on twenty-first century learning, and has taught writing to middle and high school students in California and Ohio. She is committed to furthering social justice through universal access to effective public education. Connect at *riamegnin.com*.